# IN THE DEPTHS OF THE DEPRESSION

Robert Allan Hill
Autumn, 1993

Sermons Preached at
Erwin United Methodist
Church
Syracuse, New York

WIPF & STOCK · Eugene, Oregon

Wipf and Stock Publishers
199 W 8th Ave, Suite 3
Eugene, OR 97401

In the Depths of the Depression
Sermons Preached at Erwin United Methodist Church, Syracuse, New York
By Hill, Robert A.
Copyright©1993 by Hill, Robert A.
ISBN 13: 978-1-61097-156-0
Publication date 6/1/2011

## *CONTENTS*

1. Introduction
2. In the Depths of the "Depression" ....... 7
3. Spending and Overspending
   in the Depths of the Depression ...... 15
4. A Famine of the Word? .............. 25
5. Little Ones: Children
   and God's Judgment .............. 35
6. A Good Word about Waiting ......... 45
7. On Presence ..................... 53
8. Attitude! ....................... 59
9. Open Space: Real Stewardship ........ 69
10. Tonya and Phil and You ............ 79
11. Precursors ..................... 87
12. Let's Go Home, Debbie ............ 95
13. Afterword ..................... 105

# INTRODUCTION

More than two hundred years ago, John Wesley declared: "There is no holiness save social holiness!" He meant thereby to reject an exclusively individualistic version of Christianity, and to affirm his intention to "spread scriptural holiness across the land, and reform the nation." In Wesley's view, the spheres of influence denoted in the biblical terms "sin" and "salvation" thus have communal dimensions which both engage and encompass every individual life.

This collection of affirmations of faith, based on sermons delivered from a United Methodist pulpit, stands under the long shadow of Wesley's view. Sin is a corporate and cultural manifestation of separation from God. Salvation occurs through the invasion of God's grace, remaking common life. Preaching describes the separation and announces the invasion.

The sermons as presented here are intended for two specific audiences, as well as for the general readership. On the one hand, they are offered as a gift to the congregation and friends of Erwin United Methodist Church. Preaching appears to be a monologue, but in reality is a dialogue. These sermons were born out of an energetic, tensive dialogue, in the midst of the life of a fine church. For the congregation that was willing to "preach with me," the volume is an expression of genuine gratitude.

On the other hand, the sermons are collected for students of the art of homiletics. In Syracuse, in Montreal, and at various workshops in upstate New York, students have taught me much about preaching, even as we have studied the project together. The *Afterword* contains a description of the "design" of the sermons in series, which may be helpful to fellow preachers. My own approach to the teaching of homiletics is at variance with the currently more popular "narrative" emphasis. In part, these chapters are intended to exemplify another route, a more propositional style, which I believe also should constitute an arrow in the preacher's quiver.

# In The Depths Of The "Depression"
## Text: Philippians 1:25

Many of you present this morning recall with keen memory the Great Depression of the 1930's. Over the years you have been kind enough to share your personal histories during that wrenching, perilous time. Now these your memories have also become my own, our own.

We remember pain. We remember driving through the city of Chicago in the year 1933, driving past the largest bank in the city, and seeing the door locked and chained shut, with hundreds of people outside clamoring for their money. We remember evening meals of potato soup, supper after supper. We remember migration. Families moving from the North Country to the Salt City in search of work and housing and food. Uncles traveling west to find fortune. Trampling out the vintage where the grapes of wrath are stored: the Joad family is very much our family, too. We remember seeing University families in this very neighborhood lose everything, house and savings and future. We remember as young people signing up for the CCC and sending the whole paycheck home to mom and dad and younger sisters. We remember when a church supper on Wednesday night was the only real meal midweek. We see more clearly now, with the power of hindsight, just how much damage to people the Depression did. Marriages shipwrecked on the craggy cliffs of unemployment. Educations cut short by the needs of parents. Dreams deferred and hopes lost. We remember the voice of a crippled President, for whom the word fear had two syllables, "The only thing we have to fear is fear itself."

We remember various shades of shame. The need to borrow. The need to send a child elsewhere to grow up. The need to ask a favor. The need to sacrifice one's own hope for the sake of a simple meal. Those for whom the bottle became the only path to peace. We remember when faithfulness and frugality were the same thing.

We remember heroes. Parents who did not give up or give in, but cut a path for their children. Pastors who forged ahead and built churches and taught discipline and helped the weak. Thrifty shopkeepers, hardshell businessmen, ingenious manufacturers who turned lemons into lemonade. Today, 60 years later, the pain and the shame and the heroism are very much with us.

The Depression held the life of a people by the throat, cutting the windpipe, stifling the gasps for life. The Depression killed by stealing both bread and name, and so killed the spirit. Hear John Steinbeck: "Okie use'ta mean you was from Oklahoma. Now it means you're scum. Don't mean nothing itself, it's the way they say it."[1] The Depression killed people by killing their spirits, by taking their good names, their good names won over generations, like Okie, and turning them into dirt. I doubt there is a person here, over the age of 60, who cannot recall at least one person whose spirit was crushed in the depths of the Great Depression. Look at the devastation produced when capital, financial capital, disappeared. It took a generation and a great war to recover the capital lost, and in a way it has never been recovered.

Today you and I are living in the depths of another Great Depression. We are living through another tragic devastation brought on by another loss of capital. I believe that 1993 measures the depth of this later depression every bit as fiercely as 1933 measured the depths of the earlier Depression. We are in the depths of the second Great Depression of our century, and the worst of all is, we don't even know it, or name it, or realize it. And this second Great Depression is far deadlier, far meaner, far more dangerous than its 60-year-old sister. Popular wisdom — I mean the television — for its own sake, for the sake of a simple, short, violent story will try to convince you that we live somehow during a cultural war, or in the middle of cultural wars. The comparison is then made between 1993 and 1943. The diabolical attraction of this thought, for you, is that with a war image you are given an external enemy, someone to hate, someone to fight, someone to defeat. Then, the diagnosis is simple and can be televised. *They* are the problem: the liberals, the conservatives, the assassins, the Nazis. *Those people,* as Robert E. Lee termed the Yankees, *they* are the problem. It is all very satisfactory. And false.

This is the logic that encourages harassment, abuse, and physical assault of physicians performing abortions, as a way of preventing abortion. How sweet it is simply to find an enemy, someone to hate, to fight, to defeat. And how wrong. Harder, but truer, is the recognition that the golden calf has been made from all our jewelry, that we all participate in the cultural — not war — but depression of our time, that we have met the enemy and he is us. Thus says the Lord, in the depths of the spiritual depression, "Thy people, whom thou broughtest out of the land of Egypt, have corrupted themselves." (Exodus 32:7)

As a people we have long ago spent up our moral capital, and so we are living without moral initiative. 1993 is the depth of the Great Moral Depression of our time. The banks of investment capital may be open. We may have dollars and trusts and CD's. But the door to another Bank is shut and locked and chains hold it fast. This is the Bank we have neglected for 30 years, drained of its resources and left for dead. On the door of this Bank one finds no dollar sign, but the sign of the cross. Inside this Bank one finds no plush offices or carpeted quarters, but only a kneeling rail in a borrowed upper room. Inside this Bank one finds no plans for financial growth, but only a word, a word about spirit. Across the top of this Bank, now shut, is printed a great word, *Agape.* This is the Bank of Goodness and Mercy and Love, once prosperous in this land, once full and ready to lend, once open to feed the growth of people. I tell you, look at the door to this Bank! — it is closed and locked and chained! The Bank of Goodness in America has gone bankrupt. And now we are in the depths of a real depression.

Oh, I can hear the response, a good response: Are you quite sure, Robert, that things are all that depressed? I mean, there are a lot of things wrong, but also a lot of things right. And, I guess, even in 1933 there were some who said, "It's not so bad." I expect they tended to have work, money, shelter, and protection. So today, one might think happily that there is no moral depression. One would need to forget Sara Anne Wood. One would need to forget a child run over by a school bus because the other children on the bus had never been required and taught to mind.

We lack the moral capital to build our future. We lack the goodness, the courage, the self-sacrifice, the self-discipline, the spirit of giving, the concern and care, the love of neighbor, let alone of enemy. We lack the morality, generosity and wonder. We broke the bank.

We broke it in 1966 by loving the Ford Mustang more than our Southeast Asian brothers.

We broke it in 1974 by loving our suburban comfort, fed by oil, more than Mother Nature and planet Earth.

We broke it in 1981 by loving our televisions and designer jeans more than our children's indebtedness.

We broke it in 1988 by loving savings and loan adventures more than the little schoolhouses of the land.

We broke it in 1992 by enjoying our dinners out and soft pornography and race to success more than children.

Behold the Moral Depression of 1993!

# "Depression"

I tell you this one is going to be far worse. Measure the depths of the moral depression of 1993:

A principal says to a student who wants to be a teacher, "You can do better than that."

Fewer and fewer volunteer hours remain in any community.

Twelve million children are hungry in America, the land of the free and the home of the brave but hungry.

Little corruptions of body and soul, an addiction here, a deception there, now become a tide taken at the flood leading on to defeat.

A whole generation has now come of age, "rich in things and poor in soul," without even the vocabulary with which to touch and hold real goodness.

Few poets remain.

Thanatos and Eros have so joined forces, as measured by the tragic need for 2 million abortions a year in a population of 250 million (in 10 years that's nearly 10%), that the very foundations of respect and freedom are shaking, shaking, shaking, even as we pray this morning.

Behold the Great Moral Depression, measured at its depth in 1993.

Was there ever a time that more needed the word of God? Was there ever an age, an age of moral and cultural and spiritual depression, that more hungered and thirsted for what Paul so wonderfully and generously and well calls "the joy of faith"?

(Philippians 1:25). Was there ever a time when the joy of faith counted more, when the joy of faith meant more, when the joy of faith could do more, when the joy of faith was more valuable?

You and I, together with our compatriots, persons of good will from all backgrounds and all walks of life, are called to spend the rest of our days on this earth in the depths of this Depression, even as another generation struggled with another Depression. You are those who will, over decades, sacrifice and struggle to reopen the Bank of Goodness and Mercy and Love. Banks close because of many little withdrawals. Banks open because of many little deposits. I mean not only that — face the chained bank door! — your life counts and your deposits of goodness count. I mean that your deposits, your small daily deposits into the Bank of Goodness, are the only deposits there are.

We need reminders and heroes and images of goodness. We need the "joy of faith." We need prophetic voices that ring true with a sturdy hope as we struggle in the depths of the depression. Let us tune our ears to hear their faith, and so make faith our own:

- Ben Franklin: "When the well is dry, we know the worth of water. Little strokes fell great oaks."[2]

- John F. Kennedy: "For without belittling the courage with which men have died, we should not forget those acts of courage with which men have lived . . . A man does what he must — despite personal consequences, despite obstacles and dangers and pressures — and that is the basis of all human morality."[3]

- Robert F. Kennedy: "For those of you who are black and are tempted to be filled with hatred and distrust at the injustice of such an act, against all white people, I can only say that I feel in

# "Depression" 13

my own heart the same kind of feeling. I had a member of my family killed. But we have to make an effort in the United States, we have to make an effort to understand, to go beyond these rather difficult times. My favorite poet was Aeschylus. He wrote: In our sleep pain which we cannot forget falls drop by drop upon the heart until, in our own despair, against our will, comes wisdom through the awful grace of God."[4]

- Martin Luther King: "I just want to do God's will. And he has allowed me to go to the mountain. And I've looked over, and I've seen the promised land . . . So I'm happy tonight. I'm not worried about anything. I'm not fearing any man."[5]

# Spending and Overspending in the Depths of the Depression
1 Thessalonians 2:8

You have dual citizenship: First, as people living through the depths of a moral, cultural, spiritual depression; second, as people who are followers of Jesus.

Therefore, you have a measure of existential schizophrenia. As Bill Murray put it in the film, "What about Bob": "Roses are red, violets are blue, I'm a schizophrenic, and so am I."

Nowhere is this clearer than at the point of spending, at the point of commerce, of expense, of investment.

Another generation struggled through the depths of the financial depression of 1933, with its closed banks and soup lines and dislocation. We are living through the depth of a moral depression, a bankruptcy of the spirit, in which we all participate.

Behold the depths of the great depression, sounded at its depth in 1993.

At every turn today we are tempted to give, to spend, to invest in forms of life which only deepen our malaise.

We invest in appearance first and reality second.

We invest in the short term first and the long term second.

We invest in the quick fix first and the full overhaul second.

Ironically, the three largest and tallest and newest structures in Central New York bear witness not to our cultural and moral fortitude, but to the depth of the depression around us. I mean the mall, the dome, and the casino, the structural manifestations of our spiritual malaise, all built in the last several years.[6]

We have raised a generation of children who are mesmerized, like Narcissus, by their own appearance, concerned more about what they *look* like than what they *are* like. To provide the sartorial splendor that our commercial idolatry requires, we have built *the* mall. Where do you read in the gospel that Jesus asks his disciples to be well dressed? We have spent ourselves at the altar of appearance and our youth are as well dressed as they are ill mannered. Proverbs 42:11 *(sic):* "Better blue jeans and kindness than a Brooks Brothers suit and selfishness with it."

We are captives, too, of the short-term mindset. We prefer the momentary pleasure of the spectator to the grinding discipline of the athlete. We pretend a love of sport. What kind of love, though, is embodied in a dome full of 50,000 spectators watching 22 athletes? Rows of metal seats creaking under the weight (overweight) of spectators full of dome dogs and beer. I love sports, too. But we have put the emphasis on the wrong syllable. Something disturbing lurks under the pleasure of watching.

Professional athletes do our excercise for us.

A paid volunteer army does our fighting for us. Lawyers do our arguing and thinking for us.

We invest in ease, but not in what will last. The dome is our testimony to the slogan, "Let someone else do it." We talk a good game, but we don't play the game ourselves. There is an overtone of hypocrisy here.

We live during an epoch of moral depression, when the

## "Spending and Overspending"

moral capital stored up through other generations has been dissipated, when the habits of giving and sharing once well practiced and taught have now largely disappeared. Hence we are more easily tempted to gamble.[7] The virtue of risk has given way to the vice of gambling, at many levels of life. Howard Baker in 1982 described the borrow-and-spend economic plan of that time as a "supply side riverboat gamble." The quick fix, the lightning change, the easy route have become familiar to us, even as the evidence mounts that gambling does not pay. To the east we now have a massive edifice dedicated to gambling. 450,000 people used the casino in Oneida during the first two months of its operation. Gross receipts exceed $1 million a day. College students *en route* home from Boston and Albany — our children — now stop to play the machines and the tables.

When I was nine I took piano lessons in a small farm house, as good a home and family as I have ever known. Today that farm is sold, gone, and two of the children work at the casino. From haymow and milking parlor to blackjack and one arm bandits — all in one generation.

There is money around today, unlike the Depression of 1933. But what investment do we make with what money remains? We are enthralled with a new kind of superstition, symbolized well by the Turning Stone casino.

Idolatry, Hypocrisy, Superstition. The mall, the dome, the casino. Our investment, our giving, our spending, our expense define who we are in 1993.

It would be pleasant if this cultural depression ended at the doorstep of the church, and did not also walk down our center aisle. It would be easier if we could point this finger outward, content that within the church none of this survived.

We have dual citizenship, though. We cannot remain unscathed. So, too, in the church we struggle with these contemporary demons. We confess a penchant for appearance (Paul says, "man pleasing but not God pleasing"), and a measure of hypocrisy, and an amount of superstition.

It is far easier to appear to be a good giver, than to tithe.

It is far easier to speak about the practice of the faith, than quietly to go about inviting and healing.

It is much easier to grab onto belief itself in a superstitious way ("once saved always saved") than to work out salvation day by day in fear, in trembling. There is more superstition in religion today than at any time since the Reformation.

You are here because you want to lead a Christian life, to expend and give and share in a way that pleases the God you have known in Jesus Christ. We are together, very imperfectly, trying to be a Christian church, God's own people. This, your calling, is a high calling, and a calling worthy of all the time and effort and desire which now you are giving to it. You have come here on Sunday morning to worship God. Not just to see friends or to share news or to learn something or to sing, but to sit in God's presence, and to hear God's word, which is not just a human word loudly spoken. In an age of spiritual depression like ours, only the right and regular hearing of God's word will suffice to save us from our love of appearance and our shady preference for the shortrun and our taste for the gamble.

That word today, a glorious and beautiful word, is meant to change our ways of spending. Paul, the great Apostle, writes back to one of his earliest little churches, and remembers how they lived together in those first few years after the explosion of the resurrection. First Thessalonians is my favorite letter, and I

"Spending and Overspending" 19

happily return to it, particularly in times of trial, or during weeks such as these when life is too chock full, too overfull of too much:

A newscast on what has happened to our public schools, showing an heroic principal and children who are alone in the world.

The healthy birth, against great odds, of a son.

A newscast (on national television) which crucifies one of the best people in our city — I will return to this next week.

Moments of joy in gathering and fellowship in singing and a meal on Thursday night.

As a church we have been through a time of great loss, six deaths in 10 days, each one a moment of vital need and prayer, affecting all of us far more deeply than we admit. We neither live nor die to ourselves. Occasionally there are short stretches where the water is running so fast, so much occurs so quickly and of such power, that one almost feels that one is drowning. Every loss cuts out a piece of our common flesh, and there is blood and there is pain and there is work to bind the wound, far more than usually we admit. In the course of our rejoicing with those who rejoice and weeping with those who weep, something happens which connects us to the word of God today. For Paul is teaching us about how we are to expend ourselves, how we are to invest, how we are to give, how we are to impart things one to another.

And Paul writes a remarkable sentence. I hope his word will stay with you to feed you this week, as you live by faith during a cultural depression.

"So, being affectionately desirous of you, we were willing to have imparted to you, not the gospel of God only but also our own souls, because ye were dear unto us." (I Thessalonians 2:8)

Paul has been splashing along with these little churches for 10 years, trying to keep his head above water with them.

He looks back on all that has happened.

He remembers those who came to faith.

He remembers those who afflicted him and others.

He remembers the struggles to teach basic morality to a pagan group.

He remembers the motherly gentleness all this brought out in him. Paul calls himself a wetnurse here.

He looks back on all that has befallen these folks and a powerful insight fills him and spills out into his letter.

In order to tell the truth about his experience with these folks, he uses a word he never uses again, nor has he used it before. The word is *metadidomi*, which means overgiving or overspending or oversharing or something — we don't really know what it means. It appears only a couple other times in all of Greek literature. It means something like spending squared, or giving squared. Paul is trying to spell out what I think we have also known in our experience right here at Erwin. Here it is: he realizes that in the process of sharing the gospel of God he ended up sharing his self; in the process of teaching and preaching the good news he also ended up spending his life; in the process of telling the story of Jesus he and they ended up mixing up and mixing in their lives so thoroughly that it became hard to tell where one person ended off and another began. So he uses this word overgiving, oversharing, imparting. It's the best he can do.

# "Spending and Overspending"

I believe this word of God is important for you to hear today. I know I need to hear it. Paul's word about overspending fits what I have seen here in the last two weeks. When the gospel is really shared, given, the giving carries off with it pieces of ourselves. So that a piece of me dies with every funeral. Not only the gospel, but also ourselves. A piece of you goes with every student you love, with every gift you make, with every sacrifice you offer for truth. Not only the gospel, but also ourselves. A piece of you goes with every wilful word of pardon. Forgiveness always draws blood. A piece of you gets burned up with every real encounter with Christ in others. Not only the gospel, but also ourselves.

The word of God overshares and overspends us today. Cling to that word. First, it is the gospel that God, the living God, the God of Abraham, the maker of all things, has stooped to fix up his creation, to forgive his people, to love his children. May that word be fixed in your heart. Second, it is that those who feed together on this good news should not be surprised that, at the same time, their lives, *their whole selves,* are thrown together into one.

"So, being affectionately desirous of you, we were ready to share with you not only the gospel of God but also our own selves, because you have become very dear to us."

You return into a world frought with idolatry and hypocrisy and superstition. That is the not so good news. But there is more news than that. You go also as those who have heard and lived another Reality. You know that the spending on appearance and the moment and the gamble are not real, when set beside the overspending in God which you have experienced here. Here you have been forgiven a past harmful word.

Here you have been helped over a time of craziness. Here

you have received advice that made a difference. Here others have shared your grief.

Here someone has brought meaning and purpose into a time in your life that was empty.

Here someone genuinely thought, cared, and did something, purely for you.

Here someone gave to you, in a way that cost them bigtime.

Here you found yourself in the midst of a motley crew of regular humans who are straining and pushing and jumping and pointing toward what lies just beyond words anyway, the grace of God.

Here the descendants of Paul have shared "not only the gospel, but also our very lives" with you.

That is real spending. That is the spending that finally will triumph over the moral depression about us.

# A Famine of the Word?
Text: Amos 7:13

Tuesday, July 21, 1993. Vincent W. Foster spent a quiet Tuesday morning in the West Wing of the White House. Foster was the deputy counsel, the second in command lawyer for the Leader of the Free World. Later that morning he went to the Rose Garden and watched the installation of a new FBI director. He went again to the office, made phone calls, had an upbeat talk with his boss, ate lunch alone at his desk, in front of his diploma as the top legal student in his class, photographs of his beautiful wife and young family, and photographs of his close friends from Hope, Arkansas, one of whom is now the President.

At 1:00 p.m. Foster left the office, drove to a secluded spot along the Potomac River, and killed himself.

It is not my intention further to complicate a tragedy from afar. I grieve with Foster's widow, children, family, friends. I know something about depression, and I know that Foster was afflicted by depression. I know something about perfectionism, and I know that Foster was afflicted with perfectionism. Many factors led to his demise. One powerful influence, one great north wind cutting across Foster's bow stands out, however, in retrospect. I refer to the power of the media, the power of the journalist, the power of the newspaper or television to harm, to maim, to kill.

Foster made a list, perhaps at his wife's urging, of the issues and events which were troubling him. Chief among these was the harsh, vicious, personal editorial-writing in the *Wall Street Journal*. Foster wrote: "The *Wall Street Journal* lies without consequence." Foster was deeply bothered by editorials in the *Journal* on July 14th and 19th which attacked the Clintons and their "legal cronies from Little Rock." He felt that what was written was untrue and unfair and uncorrectable. This extremely intelligent, overworked, depressed, highly committed attorney crashed headlong into one of the enduring features of our cultural landscape: misinformation and malevolence in the press. A culture that supports and sustains the kind of polluted journalism which we have today is a culture in the depths of a moral depression.

Last Wednesday night, during the Disciple Bible Study training in Binghamton, I went back to the room exhausted and ready to fall asleep early. I flicked on the TV and saw the face of our neighbor and friend, Syracuse University professor and autism expert Douglas Biklen. For the next 50 minutes I sat watching, as many of you did, and weeping, as many of you also did, while a national network personally attacked, vilified, and crucified an utterly gentle, kind scientist, whose heart and concern for autistic children knows no bounds. The scientific discussion needs to continue, and, let us notice, is of paramount interest to this congregation: to the Cambareris and others involved at Jowonio, to Sandra Challenger using facilitation in Liverpool, to children at Ed Smith School (my son's sixth grade class and his teacher Mrs. Wilson were filmed during the brutalization of Biklen), to Carol Seigart and Scott May in Australia. Let the tests continue. But why crucify individuals in the process and why put out inaccurate information in the process? The power of television lies in the capacity of an image, a few words of conversation snipped from life, a face, a bar of music, to imply, to leave a lasting impression that may be completely false, and then to race on to the next image before the mind has the time to consider, to reflect, to distinguish. Television smears people. And people lap it up.

The streams of information, from which we drink on a daily basis, are polluted.

In the year 786 BCE a shepherd prophet stood in the gate of

# "A Famine of the Word?"

the great city of Jerusalem and shouted his warning: "The day is coming when there will be a famine of truth, a famine of the word. The hardness of the hearts of people will be matched by a silence of God, a lack of right speaking, a pollution in the river of information, a famine of the word." Amos foresaw times when the accumulation of pride, sloth, and falsehood, rife in life, would harden into a verbal blackout, a famine of the word. Times when truth had no resting place, no access.

You know this in your own experience. Maybe in a friendship, when for a time there is just no way to say what needs to be said. Neither words nor ears work. Where once there was compassion and understanding, a harvest of communication, now there is emptiness, nothing to say or hear or to do about it, a famine of the word. Maybe in a family, when for a time there is just no way to address a person or a problem, a famine of the word. Maybe in a business. A dearth of truth kills more businesses than the Japanese ever thought of killing. Maybe in a church, like The United Methodist Church today, when there are some things among our clergy that just cannot be said in a way that anyone will hear. This can be a frightening time.

In the same way, Amos prophesies, as with friendship and family and business, so too with a whole culture there will come times when the fields of truth and accuracy lie empty, and a famine sends its shadow across the land.

During second year at Erwin a young man, a member of this church, a student teacher, was accused of sexual harassment by two teenage girls. He had been filling in for a gym teacher. He was bound, arrested, taken to jail. The next day his name and this story appeared in the local newspapers. Two days later the girls admitted they had lied. But the damage had been done. A later retraction on a back page was no cure for the front page photos and headlines which permanently scarred this good person.

Three years ago we had an incident in our building during which a young woman was hit by a mentally disturbed man. The article that appeared combined four factual errors with a theme and slant which harmed the church, the dance program, and the day care.

I have refused for several years to give quotations to the newspaper, unless they would interview me in person (not at 10:00 p.m. on the telephone), and then allow me to see what they were planning to quote me as having said. (This is after having three printed letters to the editor significantly altered.) This is my policy today, and it costs Erwin some free publicity, which pains me.

Before General Conference the paper tried to set up a verbal battle between me and Deborah Pritts (my future superintendent), as two local delegates with different points of view. I declined, and when I saw the so-called reporting done I was eternally thankful that I had gone home by another way.

The newspapers combine interest in veracity with interest in entertainment. Hence they focus on the marginal, not the mainstream, the conflicted and not the consensual, the dramatic but not the durable. Hence the news is more like anti-news, a negative of the real photograph.

Beware, Christian soldiers, beware. Be careful where we stop to drink. Be careful what information you trust.

In the process, individual people are maimed and crippled. The media has the power to take people's names and reputations and destroy them. "The *Wall Street Journal* lies without consequence." A famine of the word.

It would be comforting and pleasant if we could point the

# "A Famine of the Word?"

finger at discourse and communication outside the church, secure in the knowledge that inside this mighty fortress, only streams of living water flow. Pity. This is not the case. We are dual citizens, in the world though not of the world. We too carry our fair share of misinformation and malevolence.

I refer to gossip. Truly we do not know, we cannot appreciate, just how much damage our love of gossip inflicts. For the newspapers and the television tabloids have their roots in our own souls. We love to gossip. We love to pass on dramatic information, stories of conflict or failure. We love to share the juicy tidbit, all of which is utterly horrible, but not the worst of it. We do so without regard to whether what we say is true. We do so without checking our sources in person, asking those who might know and might in fact contradict the gossip. We slander people, both accidentally and intentionally. We harm, we harm. Until it has happened to you, something said of you that is untrue, and uncorrectable, you will not know its force.

Paul had it about right in describing our condition, our sin. Foolish, faithless, heartless, ruthless. (Romans 2:31-32) So we are.

In the academic world, the expression of profound doubt about the *word,* about the capacity of any printed word to convey truth, is known as "deconstructionism." This theory holds that what is not said in a writing supersedes what is said. This theory holds that what is read is more important than what is written.

Until we have become convinced of sin, we will not be ready for a word of grace. Until we have become utterly convinced of the famine of the word through which we live — the communicative form of our cultural depression — we will not be ready to hear the good news. Until you are convinced that the word of truth is as rare as a feast during a famine, you will not be ready for the gospel.

Hear this good news! In Jesus Christ God has invaded the wordfamine to bring the possibility of speech and of truth. God is at work, in Jesus, to change people, to change you, and to change cultures, to change us. With excitement and joy, Paul expresses this to the Romans, saying, "The word is near to you, on your lips and in your hearts." God has not deserted us, not left us deaf and dumb. Hear him ye deaf! Him praise ye dumb!

In 1520, a troubled monk named Martin Luther opposed medieval forms of wordfamine by affirming the power, truth, and clarity of the plain sense of the biblical word. This is the whole content of the Protestant Reformation that, on the one hand, the word of the gospel is on your lips and in your hearts, this divine word of truth. We can speak honestly and hear rightly, *in Christ*. On the other hand, in the wordfamine then and now, we suspect pollution in other forms of communication. Luther tore his beloved church apart over the word. Luther saw his personal world dissolve over the word.

God is at work to fetter tongues and to forge his future, even during a time of moral depression. God is at work to change your heart this morning, and to change your tongue this morning and to change your ear this morning, and to change our culture this morning!

Scripture has a great deal to say about speech, about the ways God is working to improve our speech even as God converts our hearts. I count some 43 direct exhortations to good speech in the New Testament. One verse may suffice for all: "Let your speech be gracious, seasoned with salt." (Colossians 4:6) Kind and honest, gracious and salty. Let your yes be yes and your no be no. Anything else is from the devil. God is at work to change our ways of speaking, to convert us to his kingdom and righteousness. Even in the depths of a spiritual depression, we can have great faith that God strengthens us to know and hear and tell the truth.

Each one of us, on our earthly pilgrimage, makes some contribution to this saintly speech, so different from the speech of the world around us, as different as the daily rhetoric of Al Childs, our recently deceased and beloved assistant pastor, was from the sickness of the *Herald Journal*. Al's saintly speech remains with us, forming, as part of God's grace, the new creation, the new speech, the new covenant. I have taken to calling Al's sayings "alphorisms."

- When someone attacks, I remember the alphorism: "I don't mind people being Christian, as long as they are nice about it."
- When someone asks about my wife, I remember the alphormism: "I am keeping her out of the taverns."
- When an institution gets something wrong, I remember the alphorism: "That's the kind of thing that gives bureaucracy a bad name."
- When I am ready to righteously attack something, I remember the alphorism, "Some things just die of their own weight."
- When someone flies off the handle I remember the alphorism, "She would be a good test pilot in the broom factory."
- I remember and repeat his nicknames for us all.

A life worthy of the calling to which we have been called is one that is righteous in speech.

In Christ, you can make a difference by changing the speech patterns around you. God is at work to remake us, starting with our tongues. Receive his gift and grace today.

The word is near you, on your lips and in your heart (that

is, the word of faith which we preach); because if you confess with your lips that Jesus is Lord, and believe in your heart that God raised him from the dead, you will be saved.

Good news, good news, good news during a famine of the word.

Yet, there is more. In Christ you can make a difference by changing the media forms around you. You can boycott newspapers you distrust. You can invest in alternative publications. You can democratize publication, especially in this era of desktop publishing! (Freedom of the press is for those who own one). As United Methodists, through Cokesbury you own your own publishing house! You can resist the temptation to believe everything you read and hear. As a community, you can demand a higher standard from the culture around you. Janet Reno has had some interesting things to say of late (I'm thinking of her criticism of "Gangster Rap"). Just as sin lives not in individuals only, but in cultures and institutions, so too God's grace is at work to change the institutions around us, to reflect the glory of God.

# Little Ones:
# Children and God's Judgment

The next time you are in Boston, take a moment to visit the Aquarium.

Ah: This is dear old Boston, the home of the bean and the cod, where the Lowells will speak only to the Cabots, but the Cabots speak only to God.

Boston, in so many ways the city of origin, the point of departure.

Boston, birthplace of the republic: Haymarket Square, Old North Church, Bunker Hill, Old Ironsides.

Boston, home to heroes: Paul Revere, John Hancock, Johnny Tremain.

Boston, where in 1838 the First Congregational Church heard a children's choir sing, "My Country 'tis of Thee." On the Freedom Trail you can talk with "Ben Franklin" attired in the garb of 1780.

On the subway you can stop at the Scully Square station and remember the man who never returned.

Take the train to Fenway Park and peer at the green monster. Try not to make the mistake of wearing a Yankees hat. Walk through downtown and the flower gardens. Spend a minute along the old streets, and feel the freshness of a country being born, being formed, being built.

Visit the children's science museum.

Boston takes the world and makes it young again!

It may be that the best spot in this young city, this birthing room for freedom, is the Aquarium. Right on the port shoreline the city has built a magnificent structure, a several-tiered tank. Coral has been transported from the Caribbean, and then also reproduced. Fish of dozens of colors, shapes, sizes swim in the blue green cylinder. Divers in fins, wetsuits and air tanks maintain the giant manmade ocean tank. Stingrays swimming in a separate pool — you could touch them! And around and around the outside of the cylinder walk mesmerized children and adults, looking on the splendor of Neptune's kingdom. There are six kinds of sharks in the Aquarium. The sand shark and others. At the top level you can watch them jump and swim. Boston returns one to the great ocean deep from which life at last emerged across the millennia. Boston takes the world and makes it young again!

On the day in which we visited the Aquarium, the place was mobbed, packed with kids and parents, classes and groups. The colors and shapes and sizes of the humans walking clockwise around the tank mimicked nicely the variety of fish swimming counterclockwise inside. I saw a little girl in dredlocks pressing her nose against the glass up toward the tank top, just as the sand shark swam by. Two Asian women photographed the coral. A boy screamed as he patted the stingray. There were maybe 3,000 people inside the Aquarium.

All of a sudden, the loudspeaker crackled. "Please be quiet, all of you." Soon the tall structure, full of children and parents, was nearly silent. The announcer continued, "I must regrettably report that a little boy is lost. He is 3 years old. He is wearing jeans and a white sweatshirt that says Boston College on the front. He has red hair. Please take a minute wherever you are and look toward the tank and then along the walkway." In a moment,

## "Little Ones"

you could feel the atmosphere in the building shift from lark to worry. Every parent's worst nightmare had hit. In the summer of Sara Anne Wood,[8] and a similar disappearance in Massachusetts, the tension around the tank was palpable. The thought that one child, even one, out for a Sunday of learning and play, would disappear, or worse, held the gathered company on a tight leash.

In a single moment, the joy of the many had been overshadowed, darkly overshadowed, by the need of just one. All knew instinctively that there are no extra children, none to spare, not one to give up, to throw to the sharks. In that kind of dramatic moment, it so very clear: every child is precious, every one dear.

I have wondered a little since then why the announcement so disturbed those of us who could see our own children. Of course you can think of many reasons. I believe, however, that one reason the announcement "child lost . . . white sweat shirt" pierced the group that day is that we are dimly aware that there is a kind of warfare being waged against children in America today.

Children suffer the effects of poverty most strongly. Children endure the effects of family demise most squarely.

Children miss the care of physicians and dentists most keenly. Children feel the impact of bad diet most sharply.

Children are too little, too weak, too powerless, too small in every way to watch out for themselves. Obvious enough. Children measure the depth of moral depression around us by measuring the amount of time, energy, commitment, and money within us, ready to be devoted to children.

This is not an easy time to grow up. Ironically. There is more money around than there was in 1933 — not enough, but more. There is more work around than there was in 1933 — not enough, but more. Yet, this is not an easy time to grow up. Ask any elementary school teacher to compare her class with ones she remembers growing up. The difficulty arises not from a financial but from a cultural crisis, a moral depression.

Last fall in a fit of short-lived determination, I began to interview parents and teachers about the conditions through which children grow today. My focus was the city schools. In 20 years, these precious entities have suffered greatly. Sixty-two percent of our city school children come out of "poverty." Leadership within our district and within our school board has been of mixed quality. Discipline ranges from mediocre to non-existent. One needs order in order to teach. So I asked some folks I respect, "How can we improve our schools?" Here is an excerpt, dated October 1992, of one such interview:

"I don't know . . . school problems go back to a breakdown in the home . . . discipline is a major, major, major problem . . . so much time is lost in discipline . . . more of the day is devoted to crowd control than to learning . . . I'm distressed . . . I consider the option of pulling out . . . but I'm torn . . . I want to support the schools . . . to go with them until it is unbearable (unbearable meaning physical danger on a routine basis) . . . the trend is away from memorization . . . writing process should be better . . . my school, to cut costs, dropped the spelling book . . . many first grade students know only 10 letters . . . I make two suggestions: 1. Parents must see themselves as teachers, become involved in teaching their children, everything from counting at the grocery store to teaching colors on car rides . . . 2. Schools and our society need to empower teachers . . . They must be given the authority to exert discipline, to say, follow my rules or you are gone . . .

"Will things change? Not in my lifetime . . . "

"Little Ones"

Most parents honestly would not believe what their children live with on a daily basis in our schools.

What will it take? Will things begin to change when finally someone dies in the school? No. That has already happened. To 15-year-old Jason Beckham. He died of complications from heart illness after being knocked down in the Nottingham lunchroom two years ago. We had his funeral right here at Erwin.

The culture around us does not honor children, does not treat each little life as if it were "made in the image and likeness of God." Otherwise, we would not have the school systems we have. Otherwise, we would not have the teen pregnancy we have. Otherwise, we would not need to have the number of surgical abortions we have. Otherwise, we would not have the vicious kinds of attacks on children which we now have.

There was a time when we actually believed that every child in this country needed, deserved a good education, and that we ourselves, in order to benefit from what Ortega called the "natural aristocracy," equally needed and deserved good, public education for all. We believed this, not in the sense that we said it, but in the sense that we gave ourselves to it. We gave our best middle class women to teaching, and many of our best lower middle and middle class men to teaching and administration. The best and brightest. We did not begrudge extra dollars spent for books and trips. We gave ourselves, as a people, as a culture, to education in a way that we no longer do.

Today we are well down the road to a two- and perhaps three-tiered educational system, which will prohibit children born poor from rising to the level of their natural ability, and so we will all suffer. Teachers and administrators have not been willing to suffer the fate of John Hus and John Wycliffe, the martyr fate of any precursor of God's truth, to communicate the horror of public education. Parents have turned blind eyes and weary backs upon the process. Things are much worse than most adults can even imagine. Five percent of the students ruin the education of 95%.

Children in the Orient today are raised with discipline, hard work, and a passion for education. Discipline to reflect the ordering power of God. Work to reflect the creative energy of God. Education to reflect the life-giving newness of God's spirit. Children are made "in the image and likeness of God."

The cultural disdain for children all around us also enters the church. As a church, we have yet to achieve the kind of caring for children which we profess. The pious words of a recent "Durham Declaration"[9] are ones we all share: "We believe that caring and providing for one another includes welcoming children into the family of the Church. As members of the Body of Christ, we know that children are gifts from God. In this we follow the example of our Lord, who, during his earthly ministry and in the face of opposition, welcomed children to his side. And we conform to the example of the early church, which, though living in the midst of a pagan empire that casually practiced abortion and abandoned children (usually to slavery, prostitution or death), helped to provide refuge for unwanted ones and their needy parents." (Didache: "You shall not murder a child by abortion or kill a newborn.") Good words. But anyone who has been around the church for very long knows that we do not completely practice what we preach, in this as in so many areas. We devote more language to love of children in church than we do actual time spent with children. Vacation Bible School (we have run one every year since 1979) is the bellwether for our commitment. Sunday School is a close second. Why is it that, when we have fellowship dinners, we forget to provide child care?

Hear the Gospel, recipients of the gift of faith. Faith like

# "Little Ones" 41

yours really counts in the depths of our social depression. The lessons today speak of measure and production, of investment and preparation, of facing down fear and facing the future with hope. Says Paul, you are children of the day!

You are sunshine people!

You are well fed at breakfast, scrubbed clean, carefully dressed, children-with-a-purpose people!

You have armor!

You have a reason to get up in the morning!

You have a reason to struggle on in the afternoon!

You have a reason to sleep soundly at night!

You have been touched by the Risen Christ!

You are God's people, God's movement for good, God's protectors of children!

You are salt of earth and light of world! You need not fear, but only watch and fight and pray, and live rejoicing every day!

In 1985 I preached a sermon titled, "In Defense of Public Education." Ground has been lost since then. But we are not free to think like losers. It is not our place to stand stiffly aside the demise of these fine schools and say, "Well, if only they all were Christian, we could win the day."

I remember Bobby Kennedy remarking about the supporters of Adlai Stevenson that they didn't mind losing. Somehow it gave them a sense of superiority, the defeated but righteous remnant. Kennedy concluded they had a love of death.

But, some will say, "I have no power. I am only a father at home watching my kids. I am only teacher. I have no power." True, but you have a voice. Remember the parable of the unjust judge? The powerless woman, using only her voice, turned power around. You have a voice. Use it.

Grace abounds here, through mothers at work, through mothers at home, through Sunday School teachers and Vacation Bible schoolers, through volunteers writing the PTO newsletter, through tutors giving time, through Daycare Center and Nursery School, through camping and college work, through children's time and time with children.

Grace will further abound once we have found a way, a structural programmatic way, of influencing our neighboring junior high and high schools. We are present every first Monday for lunch. We have a list of 10 tutors. We are outfitting our Lewis Study for afternoon and evening use.

Where will the energy and time and money come from?

People know that there are no extra children, none to spare, not even one to throw to the sharks. When the need is clearly presented, the problem is almost solved.

So it was on an August Sunday in dear old Boston, that after 20 minutes of looking and waiting, the tourists at the Boston Aquarium again heard the crackling loudspeaker, and again heard the announcer's voice, and at last heard the report: "The child is found!" The lost is found!

In that moment, several thousand people stared at one another and many fish, and cheered instinctively, just as we will as a nation stand and cheer when every child across this great land has what she needs to make a life.

# A Good Word about Waiting
Text: Amos 5, 1 Thessalonians 4, Matthew 25

Last month, Jan and I went over to the Flower City (Rochester, New York) to attend a wedding. Middle age brings some joys, including the chance to officiate at the weddings of former confirmation youth. The rehearsal was Friday at 6:00 p.m. We left later than we had planned, and drove west toward the great, fair city of Rochester (the Flower City). In the rush to hit the road, we piled robe and coats into the back seat, and settled in for the trip.

A good hour or two on the road with freedom to talk and listen can be a rare treat. The exits sped by quickly until we arrived at 490. We pulled off the Thruway and began to look for directions to the motel and to the wedding. We had some trouble locating the maps and invitations, until we remembered they were in the suitcase. Jan crawled in back to get the suitcase, but after awhile came back up front, looking a little shaken, a little pale.

We had the left our suitcase in Syracuse.

Paul Stookey said once that there are two problems with life: Sometimes life goes too fast for you, and sometimes you go too fast for life. That day we had outrun our supply lines, our mental and emotional supply lines, to such a degree that, while I murmured piously through the wedding rehearsal, Jan ransacked the nearby WalMart for socks, underwear, shoes, belts, and toothpaste.

Echoes of old voices: haste makes waste; slow and steady wins the day; only the devil has no time to let things grow; he was like a farmer who pulled up his crops every week to see if they had grown; wait for the Lord.

My argument with and for you this autumn is that we are

living through a cultural depression in 1993, analogous to the financial depression of 1933. Our sin, as the Scripture I believe would have it, lies not in various personal peccadillos first, but in the moral and spiritual structures of our time. The soul sickness of 1993, I aver, is cultural and involves us all.

For instance, the spirit of the age knows much of strawberries and little of grapes, much about spreading wildfast zucchini and little about how *slowly* great acorns grow. The depth of our cultural distress, our sin, is visible in our common haste.

Some will disagree with my analysis. One good, opposing voice — is it yours? — will want to say, "Bob, it's not that bad. Cultural malaise, but not depression." On the other extreme, another good, opposing voice — is it yours? — will want to say, "Bob, it's worse. This is not a depression, it's a war." I hear you, and surely you have some truth with you. The depression is not unrelieved. There is Erwin Church. There is public radio. And on the other hand, yes, there is violent difference between Patrick Buchanan and Louis Farrakhan. At points the depression does give way to warfare.

But I proceed. In my judgment our distress is deeper than malaise. In my judgment our condition is broader than warfare. Look for instance at just how unwilling as a people we are to wait. To pick on, somewhat unfairly, one glaring example of cultural haste:

In America today 25% (one of four) new births occur outside of marriage. Let me read through just the headlines of articles in my file on the demise of delayed gratification, the cultural eclipse of the connection between sexuality and marriage or even commitment.
1. "Mainline churches failed to anticipate the tremendous

shifts in cultural values that have undermined the well-being of children."
2. "Without being moralistic or harsh, mainline churches need to recognize that not all family forms are equal for the task of raising children."
3. "The time has come to examine the social costs of the unraveling of family life over the past several decades."
4. "No prophet, priest or preacher in history ever carried on so relentlessly about sex in all its tiresome variety as do our singers and sitcoms. Exactly what is being learned is hard to say: overall it seems to be a message which blurs the distinction between sexuality and cruelty, which glorifies death over life, and degrades humanity."
5. "Illegitimacy is the single most important social problem of our time — more important than crime, drugs, poverty, illiteracy, welfare or homelessness *because it drives everything else.*"

As a people, our hasty sexuality reflects a much deeper and broader haste, both fed and quickened by technological advance.

Too much too fast too early too soon.

Instant breakfast instant replay instant analysis instant gratification.

In this context, the church's 2,000-year-old happy report about the joy of sex and marriage has a tough time winning a hearing.

Wouldn't it be peachy if cultural haste never entered the church? Wouldn't it, though. Such is not the case, as you know. We too have our urgency. We can be impatient sometimes with those newer to the faith than we are, whose practices have not yet developed, but who are learning. Like those who know the butterfly and the back crawl and the inverted breaststroke who are impatient with those just learning to float, just learning to paddle, just learning to swim. We who worship with zeal and tithe with gusto and speak easily of faith can treat with undo haste those who are just getting their feet wet.

In the summer, I sat through another sweltering committee meeting, watching 15 people of good will try to balance a $200,000 budget. In the corner sat one of our church members, voluntarily present for another meeting, knitting something for a grandchild, a first grandchild, due to arrive. The mental picture has lingered with me. In the midst of the business of our time — we are all a part of it — this quiet, faithful, happy waiting, which somehow brought meaning and peace to the haste of the moment.

O Thou hasty post-modern Christian soul! What are you waiting for today? A job, a lover, a victory, a healing, a death, a letter, an offer, a calling, happiness, wealth, another shot at the title? Hear, if you will, a good word about waiting.

We remember our pain first. The Scripture today recalls, in three passages, the waiting pain of the community of faith in which you stand today, and by which you are saved.

Amos the shepherd prophet tells us one good word about waiting. In 786 his well-fed, fat, and sassy countrymen were speculating about the day of the Lord (when we all get to heaven, what a day of rejoicing that will be). Wait, says Amos. Good it is that the Lord delays, that God hides his full presence from us. We have not lived God's justice and righteousness. Wait, and in your waiting recall the demands of the law, that we shall love our neighbor as ourself. What a concept.

Paul the apostle in 51 CE tells his little church a good word

## "A Good Word about Waiting"

about delay. (Romans 5:2 — "Suffering produces endurance, endurance character, character hope, and hope does not disappoint." The joggers' prayer.) They had thought (wrongly) that all would be alive once the Lord came, but some had died. The work of grieving death comes and goes in waves, as many present today are keenly aware. Our cultural haste comes up out of a profound and dangerous idolatry, the willingness to make our own souls into God, and so our own time clocks into God's time clock. Jesus is coming, says Paul, with a cry of command and the archangel's call, and the sound of the trumpet, to finish the work he has begun in his church.

All in due time. Paul learned and then taught the importance of knowing how to wait.

The surprising testimony of Matthew, recalling Jesus' parable, is that the life of faith in God implies kinds of delay, and further that delay can be good. God delays, he stays his hand, he waits — and that is just the point. It makes for a long wait — and that is just the point. The wise maidens, the early feminists, appreciated the delay, recalled the psalmist shouting, "How Long, Lord?" and made preparation.

As individuals, we can cultivate the gentler arts of patience, deference, expectation. If we do so — we have not done so yet — then we will have something to teach our grandchildren and children about delayed gratification, about tithing, about prayer.

As a church, we can cultivate the cultural dimensions of patience, deference, expectation. We can plan for the future, make provision for a long wait, trim our little lamps.

Meanwhile, back a month or so ago over in the Flower City, Father Lou was waiting at the rehearsal. Three days earlier he had been sent to this parish to replace a pastor who had been removed under charges of immorality. Lou had not done a wedding in 20 years. In 1967-68 he served as a Catholic chaplain near DaNang. During his tour the nearby village priest was killed, and the Vietnamese parish asked that an American chaplain be sent to lead services, do weddings and funerals, baptize and confirm. His last direct parish experience. He showed me photographs of children in his village church, one of whom, a teenage girl, was killed by stray bullets.

Patiently, Lou led us through the rehearsal. He waited through the friendly fire of the groom's father. He dodged the shrapnel from the mother of the bride. He tested for land mines among the bridal party. He radioed in for backup assistance (from me) for the homily. He practiced the waiting, cunning delays that are a part of any serious guerilla warfare, any serious Christian ministry. In the morning, Lou lifted chalice and loaf, and proclaimed the mystery of faith, in which we wait upon God.

Ye watchers and ye holy ones . . .

Hear a good word about waiting. Milton wrote:
Who best bear his mild yoke, they serve him best:
his state is Kingly; thousands at his bidding speed,
and post o'er land and ocean without rest;
They also serve who only stand and wait.[10]

## On Presence
Text: Exodus 33:12-23, Matthew 21:28-32

1. Today we are confronted by two readings, musicians would call them scores, offered to us by the Divine Composer. Joseph Levine, Artistic Director of the Metropolitan Opera, said this week that he discovers something new every time he conducts a piece of great music. Today Moses again faces God on Sinai and Jesus again faces the religious community, and the Divine Composer meets us out of the worn pages of Scripture. It is the presence of God which we ponder now. The score is placed before us. The orchestra is ready. Now the conductor must interpret the intention of the Divine Composer. How shall we think of presence when life is so full of absence? Where is God? How shall we know that God is with us? How shall we know the entry, evidently understood by tax collectors and harlots, the entry to the kingdom of heaven?

2. Consider this. Moses wrangles with God about whether God will continue with God's people as they march in the wilderness. Moses makes his case. His people are trying to live a faithful life in a wilderness. His people are trying to remember the good in a time of moral depression. His people are trying to leave behind idolatry, to flee the golden calf. His people are trying to worship on the road.

3. Imagine this. Just when the habits of worship were all set, and the people were used to the tent and the cloud, things change. I will stretch the metaphor a little. The children of Israel had to leave the structure and safety of a sanctuary they had known and move on under the cloud of smoke and pillar of fire. They had to create a makeshift altar, an ark, as they went along for 40 years. They had to adjust to less comfort and more uncertainty.

4. I imagine that you can identify this morning with their

sense of dislocation. Any congregation that has had to move out of its sanctuary for remodeling or rebuilding can identify. Any couple who have had to pack and unpack boxes of belongings, shifting from one house to another, can identify. Any nation that has had to count the cost of overhauling huge educational and health systems can identify. Any individual who has had to move out of a marriage or a friendship or a job can identify. Any religious man, who suddenly realizes that his religion is killing him and maiming his loved ones, and who knows he must shed his pious garments, can identify. The wilderness, with its smell of drying paint, its cluttered half-full boxes of Pampers and mismatched silverware, its deficit spending, its loneliness, its religious danger, this wilderness called life can create an overwhelming sense of dislocation.

5. Moses spoke to God and pleaded, "Show us thy ways." Go with us. Be present to us. We, too, mimicking Moses, could say, "Lord, we are trying to live a straight life in a crooked time, show us thy presence. We are trying faithfully to live in a time of cultural depression, show us thy presence. We the variously dislocated Methodists of Euclid Avenue need thy presence."

6. Last Sunday evening, about 6:00, I sat drinking grapefruit juice at the kitchen table of a good friend. He went for a moment to the other room, and I sat in the quiet. Sharp sunlight fell onto the table and into the darker room behind us. Because the wind was blowing, and a leafy branch rested against the window, the light fluttered and shimmered and darted, back and forth, in and out. I sat alone there, watching the dark and light, presence and absence of light, the strange beauty of an early autumn twilight. I knew that a dozen students and Bruce were together at Westcott, that Jan and 15 high schoolers were together in Friendship Hall, that our District meeting had begun at Rockefeller, that Bishop Kim was preparing for a coming trip to Korea, that we had two hospitalized, that Bosnians were still

killing Serbs, that hunger at that moment afflicted thousands in Benin, Togo, Burkinia, Ghana, Ivory Coast, Liberia, Sierra Leone, Guinea, Guinea Bissau, Gambia Senegal, Mauritania, and Western Sahara. Not to mention Cameroon and Equatorial Guinea. I knew that unresolved differences over sexuality and political economy threatened the common good. As the sharp light flickered through the leaves and glass, and as the leafy shadows danced upon the back wall, and as two men drank grapefruit juice together, somehow a sense of presence, the absent present God of Sinai, filled the house.

7. For Moses receives God's answer, and we do well to listen with all our being to its meaning. The Lord God does indeed agree to Moses' bargain. "My presence will go with you." Meditate on presence this morning. "My presence will go with you." Reflect on presence this morning. "My presence will go with you." Come to trust in presence this morning. "My presence will go with you."

8. Ralph Harper, an unknown Episcopal priest and sometime humanities teacher from Maryland wrote a book titled *On Presence*. He wrote, "There are times when time itself seems to stop for a while and we no longer feel the conflict within us of memory and desire and the fragmented busyness of what we call the present . . . It is the same for each of us in the presence of someone who is willing to take us as we are and who offers himself or herself in return. This is an experience well-known within families, and in friendships, teaching, healing."[11]

9. In the depths as we are of a spiritual depression, such a word of grace can save us from despair. I can despair when a neighbor phones to say that her son and two others, walking Tuesday afternoon on Meadowbrook, had a long serrated kitchen knife thrown at them. I can despair when the painters report to me that a hypodermic needle lies underneath the bushes

in the front of the church. I can despair when my son reports that the morning assembly at school addressed the subject, "How to enter and leave the lunch room." I can despair when I hear that a young doctor has misprescribed a pill for someone I care about. I know the tide is rising against us.

10. But I also know that God is with us, the absent present flickering light of Sinai. "I will make my goodness pass before you . . . I will show mercy to whom I will show mercy and I will be gracious to whom I will be gracious . . . You cannot see my face . . . I will put you in the cleft of the rock." God's presence is a hidden presence, an absent presence, a backside view from the cleft rock of ages, a presence made to order for a people marching in the wilderness, worshipping a God of freedom, grace, and glory.

11. As Christian people, you believe that finally, in the fullness of time, God's presence has been pleased to dwell in Jesus, the teller of tales. You look for goodness in the figure of one who never quite made it with religious people, one who never quite felt at home among believers, one who saw through others, who "knew what was in man." This subtle Lord you have trusted or maybe just now are starting to trust. Perhaps this week you have sensed presence, in the face of a struggling teenager, in the words of a man in love, in the eyes of a woman who has been willing to risk, in the worried but honest voice of a student. Perhaps today you will connect this presence with its root and ground, Jesus, the fullness of God. And perhaps tomorrow you will tell your tale of faith to someone whom it will help.

12. For the goodness of God does pass before us this morning, crouching as we are in our little cleft of rock, and we can see in part, if not in full. Presence today blesses those who came late, those who said little, those who lacked the right appearance. Jesus contrasts one who said yes and did wrong with

## "On Presence"

one who said no and did right. He opens the door for you, opens the door of the future for you. This consort of quislings and ladies of the night seems to be holding out, jarring the door. Holding the door open. We applaud those who are labile, and have no trouble speaking about their souls. Jesus blesses those who say nothing or the wrong thing. We applaud those who have strong appearance. Jesus curses appearances, but blesses those who live right. We applaud those who come early, who stand out. Jesus loves those who at first will have none of it, who maybe for good reason have stayed apart from his vineyard for a time, but in the end come through. The latecomers, the doers, the hidden good folks — Jesus has placed himself with these — and with you.

It is not too late to start all over, and that can be exciting!

# Attitude!
## Text: Matthew 7

When the last cut had been made, and the team was ready to bear down on the pre-season practice, Lou Stark would gather his young men in a circle and tell them how things stood. His was a well-rehearsed because often-used address, smooth as beach pebbles. The Nottingham High School (Syracuse) coach knew it by heart, and relished the chance to deliver it. The older boys knew it by heart, too. It did not vary with the wind.

"Men" he began — not averse to a little exaggeration — "Men, you have now entered the toughest basketball league in Upstate New York. Yes, the toughest, the hardest, the best. This is the hardest league in which to play. Why? Because Henninger plays in the City League. Because Corcoran plays in our league. Because Central plays in our league. Because players on all these teams have the highest level of skill and desire evidenced anywhere. Because past performance has been excellent and present expectations are through the roof. Yes, for all these reasons, ours is the toughest league in which to play.

"But gentlemen, there is one other reason, too, another explanation for the fierce combat within this league. In my mind it is the most important, and you are to remember it until spring comes. You are to meditate upon it, and learn and display its truth. The main reason that the City League is so tough" — here he leaned forward, and raised an eyebrow — "the main reason that this league is so tough is that *you* are in it! You are the main ingredient, the main reason, the main agent here. Never forget it. What counts most is what counts for you. Never forget it. What happens now most depends — win or lose — on something that I cannot touch within you, your attitude, your soul. Never forget it. *You* are the reason this league is so tough!"

I have preached often enough on the limitations of positive

thinking. They are real. I have preached frequently enough on the idolatries of self-help formulas. They are legion. I have preached often enough on the social myopia of personalistic preaching. It is death. I have preached warnings aplenty about the excesses of the Little Engine that Could. They are sizable. Some Engines couldn't. Others shouldn't. I have preached often enough on the ways in which Norman Peale and Robert Schuller and Alex Carmichel (Syracuse) and others have fallen short of my humble calculation of the glory of God. They are human. My Old Testament teacher, James Sanders, referred to Marble Collegiate Church — this is 1976 — as Marmaduke Collegiate, or the First Church of Baal. We were taught to recite, as a mantra, Richard Niehbur's excellent indictment of American Liberal Theology, "a God without grace saves men without sin through a Christ without the cross from a world without death." I have done my allotted share of skewering the power of positive thinking, enough so that maybe, let us call it a corrective footnote, an inconclusive and unscientific postscript, I may be allowed 15 minutes to skim the cream from their bucket, for there is cream.

Attitude does matter.

Attitude matters, especially during a cultural depression.

For the Christian. For the non-Christian. For the religious. For the unreligious. Attitude counts. *You* count. Your mind and heart and soul are part of the league, too.

You are not a typographical error in the great script of history.

You are not a cacophonous mistake in the great score of life.

You are . . . somebody.

# "Attitude!"

You are made in the image and likeness of God. That's being human.

You are one for whom the Son of God labored, suffered, was shamed, and died. That's being Christian.

You are headed for perfection, expecting to be made perfect in love in this lifetime. That's being Methodist. Attitude matters.

Some of us — I am not naming names — yet — walk with our tails between our legs, tough when you have no tail. Some of us have found it more comfortable to assume that we do not matter and that attitude does not count. Easier, that. Easier if it doesn't really matter, doesn't really count. Hubert Humphrey in 1968, pinned this attitude on his opponents: "I know that crowd. They never saw a solution, only problems. They never saw an answer only questions. Uh uh, o no, go slow, veto! That's the Republican way." I assert that some Democrats suffer from the same disease. "Sit down, o men of God, you cannot do a thing." Some of us have forgotten our Sunday School training. Some of it needed forgetting. But some needed remembering. You are the salt of the earth. You are the light of the world. Let your light so shine before men. Some of us have found ways to slink under psychological rocks and hide out, where the rain never falls and the sun never shines. Freedom's just another word for nothin' left to lose. Come on!

Hear the good, good news. God keeps God's promises. Life in the long run responds to our best longings. God schools us in patience, in work, in risk.

Attitude really matters.

You can if you think you can! You can if you think you can! Always, no. Easily, no. Everywhere, no. Sure, you can poke holes in it, but attitude matters. Teachers see it every day. A child with a sense of ease and assurance can if she thinks she can, and she does. Another, with equal or greater intelligence, cannot. This is certain: If you think you can't, you can't. Attitude really counts.

*Ask* and it shall be given to you. If you never ask, you never get. No one knows you need. Ask. Ask. Ask. ASK! In prayer. In conversation. In letters. In business. In church. In love. Ask. There are nowhere near as many no's in the universe as you fear. Paul even says that in Christ, there is no longer yes and no, but only yes. Christ is God's everlasting YES! What is the worst that can happen? Rejection? Partial success? Or is it actually succeeding that worries you? Nothing more to complain about. Freedom's just another word for nothin' left to lose. Come on!

Attitude is everything. Asking is the only absolute prerequisite to getting.

Some years ago, at Syracuse University, a local fraternity faced a crisis. Its membership, abysmal students all, had signed on for a religion course, "The New Testament," on the bungled information that this was an easy A. The course turned out to be a blistering, miserable forced march through ancient history, philosophy, sociology, and psychology, soon nicknamed "Death in the Afternoon." The teacher was a Prussian martinet, given to high expectations, low grades and no forgiveness. As the final exam approached, the president of the fraternity gathered his browbeaten brothers and produced a plan. Last year's final exam in this course from hell had been, somehow, procured. It was a single essay question. "Trace the three missionary journeys of the Apostle Paul."

With the energy of 10 men, the fraternity president set to work. He gathered the young men in the front room. He produced maps of the Mediterranean basin. With pointer and chalk he laboriously led his doubting fraternity through the material. Ephesus. Thessalonica. Corinth. Rome. By 2:00 a.m. the war room was littered with paper and coffee, but all 20 SU students at least knew by heart the three missionary journeys of the Apostle Paul.

At the end of the review, the wisened president gave this advice: "Remember, boys, an exam is not about what you do not know, it's about what you do know! You can if you think you can."

The next morning, bleary eyed and worried, the students assembled for their moment of truth. The blue books were distributed. Imagine the shock and fear these boys felt as they read the single examination question: "Analyze and Criticize our Lord's Sermon on the Mount." A pallor wreathed the features of the patrons of the game. Slowly, one by one, the brothers rose and turned in their empty blue books, mumbling despondent words of explanation and apology. Even the president left the room, defeated, until the room was empty, except for the hated teacher and one freshman, a new pledge to the house. On his hand, before the exam, he had written, "You can if you think you can." This young one thought for a few minutes, and then, to the amazement of his brothers, who watched for a while from the door, proceeded to write for three hours.

Here, preserved in the archives of the fraternity, is what he wrote:

Dear Professor,

I ask that you judge me not according to my ignorance but according to my knowledge. Here is my essay.

I am a lowly freshman, unschooled in the ways of higher

learning, and unknowledgeable about forms of higher criticism. It ill behooves one so humble as I to criticize our Lord's Sermon on the Mount. These pearls of wisdom, from Jesus himself, are not to be analyzed with the rough hands of someone like me, but cherished, revered, and honored for what they are, the sublimest passages known to man. This course of study has allowed me to appreciate these fundamental words of our Lord.

Instead, for the next three hours, travel with me in your imagination as we review the three missionary journeys of the Apostle Paul . . . .

Attitude is everything!

*Seek* and you shall find. This passage was a hit parade favorite in the first 200 years of Christianity. In the office there are old green books that hold writings that stretch from the time of Matthew (90 A.D.) up to the creed we used at the start of the service (325 A.D.). The index shows which verses were most used by these folks, and this is one of the most popular. Seek, and you shall find! It turns out, also, that the critics of mainstream Christianity also dearly loved this passage, for slightly different reasons. Seek, and you shall find! The exact meaning was disputed. Did the seeking refer to esoteric religious teaching, or did the seeking refer to simple growth in confidence? The church fathers, as we once called them, thought the latter, a simple growth in faith. Clement: "The Word does not wish him who has believed to be idle. For he says, Seek and you shall find . . . what is sought may be captured, what is neglected escapes."[12] Irenaeus: "The Lord renders the disciples perfect by their seeking after and finding their Father"[13] (it reminds one of Odysseus on the beach, at the outset of the Odyssey, saying, "Does anyone really know who his Father is?").

The ancients thought confidence more central than

# "Attitude!"

certainty, in faith and in morals and in life. We can be confident even when we cannot be certain. Confidence is born of obedience to the commanding voice of Jesus of Nazareth, who tells us "Seek, and you shall find." (A saying also exactly so found in Epictetus and Josephus). This verb *seek* means seeking God. Prayer is seeking God if it is to be successful, opening oneself to God, allowing access to God. Life is seeking God if it is to be successful, opening itself to God, allowing access to God. So the Bible repeatedly challenges us to seek:

Seek first not food and clothing but kingdom and righteousness! (Luke 13:24)

Seek the things that are above. (Colossians 3:1)

Seek to be justified, saved. (Galatians 2:17)

Are you seeking kingdom and righteousness? Are you seeking the things that are above? Are you seeking to be made right with God? Seek, and you shall find. There is something in the very *attitude,* the intense activity of the seeking, that gives confidence of discovery. Good, good news. But you have to seek it to find it. And let the seeking be the hunt of a lifetime!

Robert Schuller once told this story:

During the first years of the Great Depression, a young man was completing his studies in mathematics at Stanford. He came from a farm in Oklahoma, and knew that there was little for him there. He knew also that one teaching job would be rewarded to the person in his class who did best on the final exam. So he sought, he studied, he worked. Even through the evening and late into the night of the exam, he labored, falling asleep on the couch. He awoke just before the exam was to start, and raced down the street, taking his seat five minutes late. The exam was one long page, and there were two extra questions printed on the blackboard. He plunged into the exam, and did his best, but the two written questions stymied him. As the exam ended, he asked the proctor if he could take home the last two questions and work on them there. The puzzled proctor agreed, and the fellow worked for two days, seeking the answer to these questions. He was able at last to find the first answer, through a long series of complicated equations, and one new insight that came to him, surprised him, in the course of his search. But the second answer eluded him. He at last turned in his exam, and made his plans to return to Oklahoma. The next day, as he was packing his bags, a voice called to him from the porch, agitated, excited. There stood his mathematics professor, red faced and shouting, "You found it! You found it! You found it! You must have come to the exam late. Those two questions on the board were two unanswered mathematical problems of our time, and you have just made history, you answered the first one!"

*Knock* and it shall be opened unto you.

For whom were these commands given — ask, seek, knock? For the Jews of Jesus' day? For his first 12 disciples? For all who were to come after them and follow him? For all people of good will? Who is the audience?

If the audience includes us, then we hear our command to stretch out and pound upon the door of the future, though for fear of what lies unknown, we are reluctant to do so.

Knock. Go on, Knock. God will be as true to you after you knock as He has been before. Of all the earliest Christians, it was Paul who best heeded this command. Knock. Go forward. Fear not. Paul lived every day as if he were just about to land in Jesus' lap. Paul raced as if he were about to cross the finish line and slump exhausted into Jesus' arms. Paul knocked on the door of

# "Attitude!"

the future *confident* that Christ who loved him and gave himself up for him would not desert him, but would meet him in the future.

We also shall live with this confidence born of obedience to the command, askseekknock.

We shall live within uncertain days as those who might just as well be "away from the body and at home with the Lord." (II Corinthians 5:8)

We shall live in the face of intractable problems, those devilish hurts that do not go away, as those who know the promise, "My grace shall be sufficient for thee." (II Corinthians 12:9)

We shall live in the spirit, remembering: "I have been crucified with Christ. It is no longer I who live, but Christ who lives in me. The life I now live in the flesh I live by faith in the Son of God, who loved me and gave himself up for me." (Galatians 2:20)

For — let us hear the good news: Everyone who asks receives and he who seeks finds, and to him who knocks it will be opened!

# Open Space
### Text: John 10:9

If you sit for a moment in the lobby of the new LeMoyne College (Syracuse) gym, and if while you sit there you are given eyes to see beneath the surface of life, you may be profoundly touched by the power of giving to create open space. A few years ago, out of respect for the selfless teaching of one Father Vincent Ryan, a group of middle-aged, middle-class Central New York Roman Catholics started raising money. They worked hard. When they finished, they built a beautiful new athletic center. Sitting in the lobby, pausing to think, one is struck by the power of an open door. Many glass doors open onto soccer and lacrosse and football fields. Tall glass windows open onto an Olympic pool, several basketball courts, four squash courts, a weight room. A gift that opens the world for others — I believe that is real stewardship. While you sit in that lobby, young people run and walk past, men and women talking together. These, at LeMoyne and SU and OCC and all over the country, are our sons and daughters. We send them off to college with hope and stern warnings. Then, they arrive and find that their socializing, on Euclid Avenue and Westcott Street, depends on their capacity to drink beverage alcohol. Among other things. The specter of hard core alcoholism among 20-year-olds in college is a very real threat. How potent, then, how fecund the open door of such a gift as an athletic center, where healthy pursuit can be combined with social life. What an opening! An open space, where young people can come in and go out and find pasture. An open space, where college students can get to know each other personally without getting drunk. An open space, where good living can supplant fear. An open space, open to healthy and handicapped alike. Wouldn't you love to be able to make a gift like that?

What strikes you about another, similar spot, this one along a lake shore several miles to our west, is the amount of green and undeveloped shoreline. Owasco Lake, like most of our Upstate lakes, now has few undeveloped lots. Yet, along this campground shoreline there is plenty of empty space. Nearly 50 years ago a handful of ministers and lay leaders, some of the key ones coming from this congregation, and led by Lester Schaff of blessed memory, spoke to a family named Case, about an old summer home on the west bank of the lake. Would the family consider giving the property to the Methodist Church? What a moment, in life, that must have been, for the one questioning and the one questioned, a defining moment. Young people by the thousands since that moment have descended on Casowasco, our church retreat center, to find faith there, and a new way to live, beneath the cross. Children, particularly many needy children, have found there a home away from home, a place of personal pasture. I am here today, in part, under the influence of this open space, open to neighbor, open to God, open to the Lordship of Christ. My own children, and yours, have had their world opened at Casowasco. A gift has the awesome power to open a door. Wouldn't you love to able to make a gift like that?

Several Sundays a year, this also may be one, a new family or two will enter our sanctuary. Do you remember how you felt the first time you came to church here? It is hard to be a newcomer. The family may come and sit midway down the aisle. An usher will offer a bulletin. The choir will sing and the minister will preach. A door is opened, a space is defined as open, there enters the possibility of communion, forgiveness, a new life. All, in part, are possible due to the giving of dead people. This church building and grounds, our two parsonages, are all bought and paid for. We have no mortgage. This space we so enjoy has been given us, opened for us, by the generations that preceded us. It has been carefully managed for effective and responsible community use. Here it is! Light, spacious, comfortable, in every corner bespeaking the generosity of those now in glory. Here it is!

## "Open Space"

Given. Beautiful. Such a gift inspires in us the idea that we may find, in our generation, different but equally potent, equally lasting kinds of gifts. Real gifts open doors. If one generation provides physical space, maybe another will provide educational and musical and emotional space. If Mildred Thomas and Hazel Spencer left us our buildings, maybe my generation will leave — what? A permanently endowed position for youth work and evangelism? A sizable scholarship fund for nursery, day care, school and college? A neighborhood needs mission fund? The sky is the limit. You will decide which doors to unlock, which lasting gifts to make. Wouldn't you love to be able to make a gift like that?

Just outside this sanctuary children are playing in the nursery school. If you have not been in the nursery school this fall, take a moment today to wander over there. Something happened in that space this summer. Something good. So much light, so much color, so much comfort, so much brilliant decoration, so much has been given to this school, this summer past. The difference is night and day. The difference is like the change from black and white to color film in the Ted Turner collection. It opens a new dimension! Real gifts release latches in life. Wouldn't you love to be able to make a gift like that?

Our city now has a new Museum of Science and Technology, a much improved Discovery Center, housed now in the old Armory. We love the imagery of this new, happy project. A place of training in armaments, including horse stables installed as far back as 1863, now will contain an exciting hands-on museum for adults and children, to teach the science of the 21st century. If you haven't met Steven Karon, director of the Museum, you have a treat in store. He is Mr. Science! He tells of a new Omni-Theatre, a wrap-around cinema so realistic that people are physically affected by the experience. A whole world of flora and fauna, of stars and fossils, of physics and chemistry is going to open up at Armory Square. All this is possible because of a gift by a man named Milton J. Rubenstein. Gifts reveal truth, expose reality, disclose information, open doors. Wouldn't you love to make a gift like that?

Still, Ecclesiastes warns us, rightly, that a generation comes and a generation goes, and there is nothing new under the sun. What has been given will decay. Others will overtake, perhaps ruin, the best of plans, the best of gifts. No amount of caution, no amount of diligence can finally completely guarantee that someone may not come along and destroy in a moment what takes a lifetime to build.

Today, as during the Great Depression of the 1930s, many of us are not inclined to give. We have been hurt by unemployment. We have been frightened by recession. We have been frozen in our tracks by the unknown future, barrelling down on us. The young couple is worried, rightly, about mortgage and children, day care and school loans. The more middle-aged rightly see college costs looming on the horizon. The mature may just have finished funding college, but now wonder rightly about health costs, nursing home bills, illness. Let's face it, there is no perfect time to start giving.

Here then is our stewardship dilemma. We know that giving opens doors. Yet we fear the future.

How hungrily we need again to feast upon the Word of God. Jesus says, "I am the door: by me if any man enter in, he shall be saved, and shall go in and out, and find pasture." What a wonderful word! In this strange word from the Gospel of John, Jesus claims for himself, acclaims himself, the open door of life. Jesus stakes his claim to the opening of doors, to the creation of open space, to the joy of pasture, the going out and coming in that real gifts allow. Jesus meets us, today, the One in whose forgiveness we will need to trust for heaven, He meets us in this judgment, that He is the Door, He the Power behind real giving, He the master of the open space, He the Lord of the gift.

You sit now in a Protestant church. You sit, that is, before the cross and under the Word of Scripture. We sit in recollection that with Luther and Calvin and Wesley came the obliteration of the line between religious and secular, sacred and profane. You sit before an altar, and above a diaper changing table. Architectural, programmatic theology. Yes, this is an arcane theological point, but it matters no end today. Jesus announces that He is the Door, the power behind giving, real giving that opens doors. Jesus asserts that in Him, in all of life, one enters and exits, one finds open space, one discovers pasture. The power and presumption of religion end in the cross. The power of giving begins with the Door to open pasture.

There is no hiding place from the Lord of the open space.
You cannot hide from Jesus Christ.
You cannot hide behind a clerical collar.
You cannot hide behind a robe.
You cannot hide in church.
You cannot hide underneath a political philosophy.
You cannot hide beneath an assertion of religious experience.
You cannot hide behind opinion, behind talent, behind wealth, behind discipline, behind shrewdness, behind commitment.

There is no hiding place down here.

There is the Door: by me if any man enter in, he shall be saved, and shall go in and out and find pasture. Luther left his monastery and taught us, by word and example, that the whole world is a monastery, holy and ready to be opened. Jesus left his seat at the right hand of God and taught us, by word and example, that every place and every person is at the right hand of God, holy and ready to be pastured.

Some years ago a group of hikers in the Rocky Mountains ended six hours of walking over narrow mountain paths, of tripping over vines, of holding the sides of slippery rocks, laden with heavy knapsacks, thirsty and hungry, by stumbling out of the mountain forest and into a wide, open meadow, a field of open grass and blue sky, a pasture. It was a moment of ecstacy. Every real gift is ecstatic, too.

Terry Waite spent five years as a hostage for the ministry of Jesus Christ. He now tells us that for four of those five years he was shackled every day, and allowed no conversation. Four years. Four years of leg irons and silence. He kept his sanity, he says, by remembering daily the service of Holy Communion, word for word, and re-enacting it in his memory in a particular place. One day he traveled to Salisbury Cathedral. Another day he broke bread at Canterbury. Westminster Abbey opened itself to him on yet another day. The power, the power of the gift of his life, given on principle for the sake of unknown hostages in a hostile corner of the world.

Gifts open doors, his gift freed hostages. Jesus, if we read the Bible right, claims to be the Lord of the open door, the Lord of every real gift. And when the door to Terry Waite's hostage cell was finally opened — that too was a moment of ecstacy. Every real gift opens doors.

The central fact of all of life is now within earshot. May we today have ears to hear. At the center of time and space and all things visible and invisible stands one Jesus of Nazareth, the gift of the Father's unfailing grace. To us Almighty God gives this Jesus. Jesus, to whom the Psalmist prayed, "O Lord open thou

# "Open Space"

my lips . . . Open mine eyes." Jesus of whom the prophets dreamed, "He shall open and none shall shut . . . he shall open the eyes of the blind, bring the prisoners out of prison . . . bring all the tithes into the storehouse . . . and see if I will not open for you the windows of heaven." Jesus, who touched the deaf man and cried "Ephatha, which means be opened," who touched blind Bartimaeus today and gave him sight, opened his eyes, of whom the disciples after Easter on the road to Emmaus did say, "Did our hearts not burn within us as he opened to us the Scripture?" Jesus, in whom Paul trusted, as he wrote, "A great door is opened to us . . . pray God will open to us a door of utterance." Jesus who cries out to you today: "I am the door: by me if any man enter in, he shall be saved, and shall go in and out, and find pasture."

Jesus is the Door, He the power behind every real gift, He who opens space through giving. He uses religious people, sometimes. He uses unreligious people, sometimes. He claims for himself the mantel of Lord of the gift. If we are called to be his people (and let us at least mention the possibility that not all may be so called), then we will be mixed up in giving. Real giving. Gifts that do more than salve the conscience. Gifts that open doors.

Today the Door, the Gift of the Father's unfailing grace, is reported through his giving, to have made the blind see. I believe this miracle, because I have seen him do the same this week. We began at the LeMoyne gym, and there we may as well end. If you go to the athletic center about 5:00 p.m., you are likely to see the doors open for a young woman walking with a white cane. She comes by bus. Bus drivers can open doors with kindness. She walks through accessible paths and halls. Architects can open doors with skill. She finds her way to dressing room and pool. There is still room in life for a neighborly helping hand. She walks past basketball courts where two teams in wheelchairs play. A little thoughtfulness by an administrator can open a door. She further passes a room set aside for older, weaker folks. Some alumni remembered grandpa, and opened a door. By herself, with her white cane she walks into the pool area, puts down her towel, greets the lifeguard, feels her way to the diving board, climbs, walks, toes the end of the long board, bends, arms over her head — I tell you real giving opens doors! real giving brings sight to the blind! Jesus Christ is the Lord of the gift! — she pauses, it is an ecstatic moment, and then with trust and thrust she dives, and swims, alone, and free, free to go in and out and find pasture, and blind and one who receives a kind of sight, through gifts that open doors.

Let's open a door or two this year.

# Tonya and Phil
Text: Philemon

You will have by now, no doubt, surmised that I am a strange person, given to predilections and delights as a group altogether out of the ordinary. I enjoy worn out cars, sardines, one sport coat at a time, frugality, bridge, late evening, Sinatra and Bennett, lasting if not easy friendships, older and nobler professions, city homes, Woody Allen. I also enjoy winter. I am increasingly out of control. Only regular contact with the public, through the rigorous practice of ordained ministry, keeps me from becoming totally unreachable. I owe my sanity to the Christian church. Thank you.

So, it is not wholly unfathomable that, when I consider the story of Tonya Harding, my first thought is of Philemon, Paul's shortest letter. Hence, today's sermon. Especially today, during the depths of a cultural depression, we need moral lessons that will aid us in our daily living.

I began to love the Winter Olympics in 1980, the first winter of fatherhood. We lived then in a little Cape Cod in Ithaca, two bedrooms and a porch. The games were held in Lake Placid. They were spectacular. In 1984, we watched the games from the living room of a rambling old country house, about an hour from Lake Placid. That year, the skating began to eat away at me. My wife was once mistaken, in Lake Placid, for Dorothy Hamill. The Winter Games in general, but the skating, ice dancing, in particular started then to haunt me. Courage is grace under pressure, and courage is the meaning of faith, and courage is the marrow of freedom. The skater is alone, straining against nature, a fitting image for the heroics of life, life as life is meant to be, freedom, I am that I am, God. Give me the solo first and the chorus second. Give me the boxer first and the rowing team second. Give me the sermon first and the seminar second. Give me the poem first and the party second. Give me the skater first and bobsled team, Jamaican or American, second. I love to watch the skater. Although many, Philistines all, will not agree, Tonya Harding as a skater brings a strength, power, athletics, and verve to ice which is new in American sport. Skates laced, music playing, silence over the patrons of the art, she is a bird in flight, Barth's word for the Gospel. So much of religion unintentionally kills the human spirit. Of course I believe that love without marriage can be wrong. But I am sure that marriage without love is immoral. (Just an aside). She is perfection, art in life, over the ice.

Thus, the journalistic depiction of her off-ice performance, some of which may be true, jars by contrast. One so graceful on ice is so graceless in life. One so disciplined on ice is so wayward in life. We like our stories tidy, not messy. In her 20s, Tonya Harding reminds us that it is much easier to grow a body than it is to grow a heart, much easier to exercise the legs and arms than to fetter the soul.

I hasten to add that I am speaking of the-media constructed Tonya Harding, not of the girl herself. We have little to no way of knowing, yet, much about the real person. Learning about Tonya Harding from *20\20* is like learning about First United Methodist Church from Vince Golphin. Laughable.

In the media representation, young Tonya is a runaway fugitive and thief. She has a bodyguard. No comment about the bodyguard. They are accused of trying to steal a gold medal by hobbling her opponent, hence the thievery. She is described as a poor person, enslaved economically and educationally, hence her status as a fugitive. Like much of what happens in ordinary life, this one-dimensional hit and run journalistic creation, Tonya by TV, is riddled with tragedy. Grace disgraced. This is why her story is so compelling.

# "Tonya and Phil"

You know about things going wrong. Life begins and ends with troubles, with tragedy. Upon the winter ice of tragedy blows the warmer wind of God's love, the gospel of Christ, set forth again — let us pray it not be pearls before swine — in Paul's letter today.

Here Paul tells about that which refreshes the heart. His short letter opens a window on the anatomy of forgiveness. In prison, Paul met a fugitive thief named Onesimus. He befriended the runaway slave, and by accident learned that he, Paul, also knew intimately Onesimus' owner, Philemon, or Phil, for short. Paul, Onesimus the slave, and Philemon the owner. In short order, Paul learns that Onesimus has stolen money from his master and has run away to Rome, where Paul meets him in prison. Paul sees an opportunity for reconciliation, somehow procures the thief's liberty, and sends him back — no small thing — to meet his master, whom he has wronged. Onesimus is trapped, a condition of life, in a wrong he has committed. There is no way to wriggle free. Although he is on the run, he is more a slave on the run than he was with his master, because he has chained himself to the tragic rhythm and wheel of life. And so have you. And so have I. And so has Tonya. We exempt from this sermon those who have never harmed another person, who are still coated in the "original blessing" of creation.

The scripture shows three people involved in the anatomy of forgiveness. It shows the fugitive, Onesimus. It shows the friend, Paul. It shows the victim, Philemon. It speaks to us today of God's good and loving purpose in life, that which refreshes the heart. Onesimus cannot free himself any more than Tonya Harding can free herself from the past. I find it unutterably significant that the media can tell the story of Onesimus or Tonya, fugitives and thieves, so repeatedly, with no reference, in this or in other similar stories, to the modern equivalents of Paul and Phil. Onesimus cannot free himself. Tonya cannot free herself. But Phil can free Tonya, or Onesimus, or anyone else who has harmed him, by God's grace, *and with Paul's help.*

The real Olympics of life are not only or mainly on the ice, but are played out daily in the home and office and street, as fugitive and apostle and victim, when inspired, seek forgiveness.

Phil, Paul's friend, was a person who "refreshed the heart." Wouldn't you like to be a person like Philemon, of whom the crustiest and saltiest of religious fanatics, Paul of Tarsus, could openly and repeatedly say, "He refreshes the hearts of the saints"? He refreshes the heart. Onesimus was discovered by Paul and forgiven by Philemon. Paul does not command Phil to forgive the debt. He rather suggests. He does so because, let us remember it, he argues that only good that is chosen is real good anyway. Paul trusts that in God's time even things done in malice are made to serve good. Paul intercedes. He intercedes for Onesimus. I wonder how often we notice the times when it lies in our power, with a short letter or a phone call or a suggestion, to intercede on someone else's behalf. Paul could do for Onesimus something the fugitive could never do for himself, gain him a hearing before the one he had wronged. Paul could open a door, through which, with courage, Onesimus could walk and regain his freedom.

I make this complaint against myself, my church, my world. Too often we see tragedy only from the eyes of Tonya or Phil, Onesimus or Nancy Kerrigan. We see the thief. We see the victim. But we do not see, or take the time to see, that someone can intercede. Someone can speak an intervening word. Paul did. I tell you, when you are in that third position, you have a power to do what neither Onesimus nor Philemon, neither Tonya nor Nancy, can do for themselves.

Today I ask you, sisters and brothers in Christ, to look around the prison house of your life and notice those who may need your intercession. You may hold a key for someone, a key very easy for you to turn, perhaps even as inconsequential as the writing of a short note, a letter of introduction, done at the right time, in the right way, for the right purpose. You may not be the victim, and you may not be the thief. Watch, you may hold in your hands, to be used in faith, the means of grace for another's deliverance.

It would take another kind of gold medalist to free Tonya. Sure, I can fantasize. Someone who knew both Harding and Kerrigan exceedingly well. Someone who had taught them faith by speaking and example. Someone who could recruit Nancy Kerrigan to speak in favor of her assailant, to radically forgive. It staggers the mind, like any real moment of forgiveness. A pipe dream, but wouldn't it be wonderful?

John Wesley loved Philemon, which speaks he said, of "how Christians ought to treat of secular affairs from higher principles."[14] It could happen for Tonya. It would refresh the heart.

John Calvin respected Philemon, noting that "God's elect are sometimes brought to salvation in unbelievable ways against all general expectation by devious means and through labyrinths."[15] It could happen for Tonya. It would refresh the heart.

Nicholas Berdyaev knew the meaning of Philemon: "We need a heroic love of freedom, which lays stress upon the value of every human creature."[16] It could happen for Tonya. It would refresh the heart.

Sometime this week you may be in the third position, Paul's, able to intercede before a victim on behalf of a fugitive. I pray your spiritual skates will be sharpened. I pray your spiritual leg muscles will be toned. I pray your spiritual balance will be set. Then, when that moment comes, you can circle the rink and gather yourself and in the power of grace hurl yourself into a triple twist, and land without a fall, having interceded for another. Of you, then, we can say, as Paul did of his friend Phil, "That fellow refreshes the heart."

Happy skating.

# Precursors
Text: Mark 1:1-8

1. Early this fall public television carried an account of the Oregon trail. I have forgotten most of their report, except the photograph of one rugged pioneer. This tall man, shabbily dressed, with beady fiery eyes and hair coming out of every pore in his body, apparently finished the trail. After a long summer of heat, of danger and mishap, travelers on the trail finally had to end their hike to the Pacific Ocean with a few days of bushwhacking through the thick undergrowth which led from the mountains to the open coast plain. Every group of travelers endured this final gauntlet, until our hero, the hairy tall pioneer, took it upon himself to cut an eight-foot-wide path through the forest, for all future travelers to use. He received no pay, nor any notoriety, nor any other benefit. Dressed in denim and animal clothes, covered with hair and beard, possessed of and by a certain vision, this precursor of the American West cut a fine forest road to finish the Oregon trail. What a gift to the future! And yet, fascinated as I was by his heroism, for the life of me, I cannot remember his name.

William Tecumseh Sherman remarked: this is the fate of the soldier, to die a hero's death on the field of battle, and have one's name misspelled in the newspaper.[17]

One day last summer, my daughter Emily and I went over to Fay's Drugs to fill a prescription. Ah, Fay's. Why is it, with all the great, much ballyhooed variety in product available today that we still spend most of our money at Fay's and Peter's? We made our request of the pharmacists, and stood aside to wait. It was a rainy day, a day for meditation, a day in which Syracuse excels. We looked through the magazines, counted the number of aspirins, listened to the Christmas music on the house radio — they start that on the fourth of July — and waited, and waited. Waiting is the hardest of work. While we waited, a little old lady

— sorry, Jo — approached the pharmacist, dressed in damp slicker and wearing a leather belt, with whitened hair and a gleam of fire in her eye. We perused the magazines: *Newsweek* and *Cosmopolitan*. Then the pharmacist called this drenched woman's drug before ours: "Schiess, your prescription is filled. " Hark! I stumbled over to the register and complicated the already complex computerized payment for the medication (It reminds me of the cartoon: "The computer is down, so we will both save 20 minutes.") "Are you the Rev. Betty Bone Schiess?" I had never met the woman, although I have assigned papers about her and mentioned her and thought of her. She was one of the first Episcopal women ordained priest in 1975, and she has lived in or near our neighborhood for many years. I identified myself as the pastor of Erwin Church, which did not lessen the skepticism with which she viewed my assault on the cash register. She brightened up, though, when I asked to introduce her to Emily. As she left, this comment floated our way: "So — one day you will be a Methodist Bishop," said the Rev. Schiess. (She was speaking to Emily.) Afterward, excited, I pounced on the cash register attendant, demanding to know if she was familiar with the Rev. Schiess, precursor of women's ordinations, a neighborhood legend. "You mean that old lady in the umbrella and rain bonnet?" Yes. To die a hero's death and have your name misspelled in the papers. Just so.

Such is the fate of those who cut the trail, those who pave the way, those who prepare the way, the precursors of the present. Miguel de Unamuno once wrote, "Truly in a lifetime we do not know the good we do."[18]

I have not had the chance to read the *Satanic Verses*. The book's author, Mr. Salman Rushdie, lives every day wondering whether it will be his last. He is an Indian of Islamic background, educated in Britain, who had the temerity offensively to write about the Koran. Now he lives in a cultural wilderness of his own, haunted by fear, the embodiment of the price of free speech in our time. I care about Salman Rushdie. It is no easy task to try to say something honest and true in our time, particularly when the subject is religion. As a preacher, the closer one comes to truth, the more pain and anger one ignites.

Now Rushdie lives on a daily diet of fear and resentment, locusts and wild honey, paving the way for the interaction of Islam and the West, cutting a new trail.

Abraham Lincoln, no stranger to uncut trails, put it well in his second inaugural: "One does not easily win men's applause by comparing their actions to the purposes of Almighty God."[19]

I wonder. Have we yet acknowledged the important precursors to our own faith and life? Have we met John the Baptist, in our own life and faith? Have we realized that we ourselves, at our best, are only John the Baptist writ large, preparing the way for the Lord?

If so, we have read or heard read today's Gospel. The beginning of the good news is: camel's hair . . . leather belt . . . locusts and wild honey. The beginning of the good news is: call to repentance . . . offer of forgiveness . . . baptism. The beginning of the good news is: unpleasant events . . . uncomfortable words . . . prickly people. The beginning of the good news is: struggle as a precursor to love . . . pain as a precursor to truth . . . fear as a precursor to the courage of faith. The beginning of the good news is: John the Baptist, preparing the way, in camel's hair, locusts and honey.

Very unwillingly do we accept the importance and role of the precursor. Forgotten is much of the heroism of the precursors, those who cut the trail, paved the way, prepared the way.

We remember Martin Luther, and John Calvin and John Wesley, the Protestant founders, who all finally lived long and fruitful lives. We forget John Hus and John Wycliffe, burned at the stake, dying a young man's death, paving the way for Luther and Calvin and Wesley. We remember Martin Luther King. We forget Medgar Evers, dying a brutal death in Mississippi, dying a young man's death. We remember George Washington, but forget Ethan Allen. We remember Ulysses S. Grant, but forget John Brown.

The beginning of the good news, in your life, comes embodied in those events and people who pave the way for grace.

The holidays can perhaps teach us this. After some 15 years in parish ministry, I have now a great catalogue of memories of holiday events, which though painful can be precursors to grace. What is it about the holidays? These weeks from Thanksgiving to New Year's provoke the most unusual explosions in personal life, in family life, in church life, in community life. Explosions, let us say, of the thermonuclear family. These can be frightening events, harsh and discomfiting. These events at first do not seem like good things, beginnings of the good news. Sometimes, in fact, they are not. But often enough they become doors opened into new and better life.

I remember explosive holiday disagreements over church decisions, which led by grace to closer friendship and better ministry.

I remember explosive holiday meals and parties, garnished with anger, envy and resentment, which led by grace to good fences at last constructed within families. Good fences still make good neighbors.

I remember an explosive Christmas Eve visit in a barn, a

fitful argument over the worth of marriage, which led by grace to a stable family.

I remember an explosive New Year's dinner: roast turkey, giblets, dressing and verbal warfare, sister upon sister, which led by grace to maturity, distance, and peace.

I remember explosive choir rehearsals, painful attacks on the director, which led by grace to a more realistic assessment of the church and its life.

In our first parsonage, there was no office, nor was there a pastor's office in the church. So when the need arose for personal counseling, this was done in the living room. Jan would take our one little child upstairs, and wait. One Friday late afternoon just before Christmas, I spoke again with a woman who was deeply distressed. Depression is a real enemy, especially at this time of year. We Christians bear an awful guilt for the latent cruelty of the holiday season. Experience just never measures up to expectation at this time. Toward the end of the hour, it must have been something I said, this good woman rose from her chair and addressed me with the most colorful, novel, and adult string of four letter words that I have ever heard. Her rhetoric would have made a sailor blush. She took her coat and went through the front door, when all of a sudden Jan came pounding down the front stairs and shouted, "Don't you talk to my husband like that!" Do you know, that woman came to our home for Christmas breakfast? She apologized, appreciated, moved on.

Have we appreciated the difficult events in life which sometimes are precursors to grace?

The beginning of the good news, in your life, comes embodied in those people and events, who are precursors to grace.

This is good news, for you as a parent, as you see so much of your life given over to cutting the path for children.

This is good news, for you as a brother or sister, as you see some of your life given over to cutting a path for siblings.

This is good news, for me as a pastor, as I see so much of my life given over to cutting a path for future ministries, the fruit of which will not be seen for years. (I think often of my predecessor, Mr. Rush, who paved the way for much of what has happened at Erwin since his departure in 1984. Don's first sermon from this pulpit — how many heard it? — was interrupted by a group of members, fundamentalists, who sang, "Spirit of the living God, fall afresh on me." All those folks have since left, but not without a lot of work, a lot of struggle, a lot of pain.)

As a matter of fact, this is good news for us all the time as Christians. We are not Jesus Christ. In that little statement is much of the outline of Christian living. We have met the Lord and he is not to be mistaken for ourselves. The church, our church, is meant to prepare the way of the Lord. The beginning of good news. We are to create an environment, or a collection of environments, through which Christ can enter human hearts. Much of this involves just getting out of the way. We can more easily block people from Christ than we imagine.

Behold the Baptist, precursor. Dressed in camel's hair and leather belt. Eating locusts and wild honey. Preparing the way of the Lord, making straight his paths. Behold him in events in your life. Behold him in people in your life. Behold him in your life.

Precursors teach us the courage of real faith. So much is said so easily about faith in sermons like this one. Real faith is courage in difficulty. May God give you such faith. In such faith is the meaning of life.

Martin Luther wrote, "It is impossible to understand faith unless one has at one time or another experienced the courage which faith gives a man when trials oppress him. But he who has had even a faint taste of it can never write, speak, meditate, or hear enough concerning it. It is a spring of water welling up to eternal life."[20]

# "Let's Go Home, Debbie"
Text: Matthew 25: 31-46
(November 21, 1993)

These gray days, late autumn days, with shifting light and shadow have always held, for me, an uncanny significance. Something in the naked tree limbs, grasping empty gray. Something in the crisp air, foretaste of the Ghost of Christmas Future. Something in the constant twilight. Dr. Chirevo Kwenda's dissertation defense at Syracuse University on Tuesday included, if I understood it, a reference to the sacred in the world. Something of that cosmic sacrality lurks behind the dark maple limbs of November. At least for me.

On this occasion, on this date in history, the naked tree limbs, crisp air, uncertain light recall the violent death of a young president. Television and modern American violence have grown up together over 30 years. Women and men of my generation know where they were on November 22, 1963, like those of another generation recall December 7, 1941. They remember the hour the message came, the people who delivered the word, the reactions of family members, the atmosphere of the day, the hidden meanings, unspoken words, portents of the future which all were somehow connected to the dark maple limbs of that November. One remembers: the flag-covered casket, borne by a simple wagon, drawn by a team of horses; crowds of mourners; women's black hats; children waving; school flags at half-mast; bewilderment, anger, fear, grief. An English teacher, reciting Whitman's 100-year-old eulogy for Lincoln:

> O Captain, my captain, our fearful trip is done
> The ship has weathered every rack, the prize we sought is won
> Exult O shores, and ring O bells
> But I with mournful tread,
> Walk the deck my Captain lies,
> Fallen cold and dead.[21]

I know that many of you still can feel, can taste the trauma of those days. Days in which a hard and bitter truth flew home, came home to roost. The violence in which America was born now haunts the land of the free and the home of the brave. Violence.

Pioneer's violence against natives.

Plantation owner's violence against slaves.

Soldier's violence in restoring the Union.

Overseer's violence against workers.

Rumrunner's violence against authority.

The lesson of the Kennedy assassination was, and is, that the violence in which America was born lives on, and will turn its wrath upon future generations. The Boston patrician's death in the south, in a former slave state, in Indian country, on the old western frontier, was a moment of apocalyptic judgment upon a nation, which is still soaked in violence.

Today the cultural depression through which we live finds its apex in the tide of violence overtaking our land. Ours is a culture soaked in violence.

European tourists avoid the highways in Florida. Congress seriously considers utilizing the national guard in the capital.

More people die on our roadways in one year than died during the whole Vietnam war.

One — perhaps the only — feature which all sides of the abortion debate today seem to have in common is a penchant for violence — violent rhetoric, violent attitude, violent action. The community of women and men today is torn, visibly so, in the raging debate over rape on and off campus.

High schools erupt in riotous, random destruction. A 30-year-old female teacher in Syracuse is beaten repeatedly, severely by a student. A look is grounds for a fight. A word is grounds for a beating. An argument is grounds for a killing.

I'll get my lawyer and sue you.

I'll get my representative and do you in.

I'll get my friends and screw you.

I'll get my gun and kill you.

An elderly gentleman has lived in a home for 50 years. There he and his wife raised two children. There a family slept, ate, talked, grew, loved, learned, prayed. A home is a sacred space, when it is a real home. Finally flesh begins to give way to spirit, and he is hospitalized. The house is empty, dark, for the first time in a long, long time. Three nights later somehow breaks through the back door and steals a few items. The space, the place of home and hearth and caring has been violated — it is a sacrilege — for the sake of $300.

Our culture is fallen deep into sin. Our habits of spending, our impatience with waiting, our forms of communication, our treatment of children, our lethargic stewardship, our treatment of enemies, our disregard of precursors — they all convict us. Surely you must be convinced of the presence, reality, force of sin!

Key Bank is open. Fleet Bank still serves us. OnBank opens its door. But there is another Bank today whose doors are chained and shut. The bank of moral capital, the bank of cultural grace, the bank of goodness and mercy in this land is bankrupt. Too few deposits, the spiritual fruit of right living, have been made since November 22, 1963. It will be another generation before the bank can open again, if it ever opens.

Nor are the hallowed rooms of Erwin Church, or any church, free of violence. Our capacity to differ, with courtesy, never fully developed, is today at a particularly low ebb across the denomination. At General Conference I witnessed the beginnings of a further stage of subcultural disintegration. One day for 50 minutes gay and lesbian protesters raised a din of noise and shut down the conference. The vote over Religious Coalition for Abortion Rights, split by less than 5% of the delegates, became a vituperative exchange, men vs. women, liberal 50-year-old women vs. conservative 30-year-old women, South vs. North. This week our church newspaper reported a particularly rancorous meeting in Ohio. Nancy Yamasaki of Seattle said: "I have not seen an inclusive process. All we've seen is Euro-American males up there making decisions."[22] A veteran minister resigned the leadership of an important task force. I telephoned him in Columbus on Friday, and heard the voice of a caring person, deeply troubled by divisions of gender, race, theology, and age. "It hurts," C. Joseph Sprague said. Violence hurts.

Our culture is soaked in violence, and those of us in the church have some damp clothing, too.

Once you are convinced of the power of sin, you may be open to hear another word. Once the horror of violence hits home, a new door can open.

In 1956 John Ford dramatically described this turning in his movie, "The Searchers." The film tells the story of a young girl,

## "Let's Go Home, Debbie"

named Debbie, who is captured by Comanches. Her uncle, a Civil War veteran, and brother set out to find her, against the backdrop of the great American West, but more importantly against the background of violence in America, violence of race upon race, gender upon gender, region upon region. Throughout the film, John Wayne's greatest role, it is clear that once Debbie is found she will be killed. She must be killed because she has been violated. She personifies the innocence and youth of a people headed west, the mythic goodness and mercy of the pilgrim origin. The violence required to build the country has ironically ricocheted and hit her. She has been forcibly raped. Her uncle intends to kill her rather than bring her home, rather than live with the constant reminder of violence, and the shame of its consequence.

The film ends with her escape, the slaughter of her Indian family, and with her uncle towering above her, ready to rid the earth of her violated soul. But something has changed in his heart. The very sting of violence, brought home to him, somehow has caused him to know mercy. At some level, I believe the film suggests, the uncle knew that this violence had its root in our own violence.

As the title of the sermon indicates, he stoops to her, and gathers her up, and says, the last words of the film, "Let's go home, Debbie."

This same dilemma still faces us, as a nation, as a people, as a church. We have our share of Debbies. We can respond with further violence. Or, we can begin to go home, day by day, to suffer the shame and dishonor which all violence finally bequeaths, and in Christ learn to practice the ways of peace. Living day by day with the hurts and victims of the enemy's rapacity is not easy. Living hour by hour with the violence of 1993, which has its roots in 300 years of history, is not easy. I would argue that without the cross such living is not even possible. Much easier, the quick slaying than the laborious long march of mercy. But so much truer and better, the gospeljudgment today, the Christian path of non-violence.

For Jesus teaches us the way beyond violence. He gives two preliminaries, and five practical commands. Let's go home, Debbie: roll up your spiritual sleeves with me for a minute, and work with the gospeljudgment!

Preliminarily, Jesus reminds us that we face judgment, an accounting, a reckoning. This is not news. Life itself spells this out for us. Old age, dusk, autumn — we know in our bones about accounting time. Harvest, report cards, evaluations, income tax — we know in our experience about a judgment time. Jesus calmly reminds us of this, with two more novel items. First, he tells us that we will be judged as nations, for our common, our collective lives. Here he says nothing about individual reckoning, only the nations. Second, he connects judgment with human relations, not with religious experience. In the judgment, heightened religious experience counts for nothing. It is actual living, not religious experience, which is judged. Service, not music not retreats not fellowship not ecstacy not preaching not prayer. Service, refreshed by religion.

Jesus gives us five forms of exercise for those preparing for judgment, all of which are measured by their effect on the weakest members of the church and of the human family.

Find a way to sit quietly with those who are imprisoned. With those imprisoned by fear, by pride, by ideology, by personality, by circumstance. Go and sit with them and listen.

Find a way to heal sickness. Health is too important to leave to the doctors or even to Hillary Clinton. You go and heal.

Assess what habits have brought you health and share them.

Find a way to cover the naked. Those who are exposed, open to harm. Exposed to scorn to mocking to criticism to false judgment. Go and put some clothing on them, some encouragement, some humor, some honor. Go on, it's part of the way home.

Find a way to befriend strangers. Strangers need welcome, friendship. Until you've been one, maybe you don't know. Watch for the stranger and offer hospitality.

Find a way to offer food and drink, not to those who already have plenty of both, but to those who have parched throats and empty stomachs. How we would love to take pitchers of faith and loaves of hope and batches of love to all of the people in our very neighborhood who hunger for them. May God help us to find a way.

These are the things that make for peace. These are the signposts on the long road home from violence. These are the gospeljudgment words. A church which practices them, and is practiced in their arts, will have much to offer the healing of a violated culture.

In August we visited Hyannisport, and there walked around the Kennedy memorial. It is a moving experience. The harbor is laden with beautiful sailboats. The monument is handsome. Across the round deck of the memorial there is chiseled a sentence quotation: "I believe that America should set sail, and not lie still in the harbor." Kennedy, at his best, appealed to our honor, and not to our security ("not a set of promises, but a set of challenges"). It is our honor and our willingness to sacrifice, which will moderate violence ("ask not what your country can do for you"). It is our stamina which will make the difference ("to bear the burden of a long twilight struggle, year in and year out, rejoicing in hope, patient in tribulation").[23]

Much of what Kennedy hoped, has been achieved. Communism in dead. Nuclear weaponry is under control. Relations between Protestants and Catholics are good. Basic civil rights have been guaranteed. A man has landed on the moon. Latin America is opening up to us.

But the cultural violence which ended his life rages on and on and on and on and on . . . . . .

Let us go home, steal away to Jesus, wage peace as we approach his judgment.

Let us be willing to "pay any price, bear any burden, meet any hardship, support any friend, oppose any foe" to heal this land of its violent heritage.

Let's go home, Debbie.

# AFTERWORD

Two didactic comments are appended here.

First, as rhetoricians have long known, design is everything, in speech as in architecture as in life. Sermon design is the single most important facet of sermon preparation, and at the same time the least understood and most poorly taught feature in homiletics. The shape of the sermon should "spell" the sermon without the sermon. Today, narrative and television have almost eclipsed real design. (And non-design, or stream design, can occasionally be effective.) But most speakers and most preachers need the support of good design. Grady Davis and David Buttrick bear re-reading.[24]

The sermons in this volume have a single, hour-glass design in common (with a couple of exceptions). Imagine an hour glass. The top of the glass has a wide upper part and a narrow lower part. The bottom has a wide lower part and a narrow upper part. Separating top and bottom is the neck of the glass. The sermons in this book use this design. The top of the glass, the first half of each sermon, describes sin, first manifest in the culture (upper top) and second manifest in the church (lower top). Sin is easier to see first outside ourselves (culture), and then gradually to admit within ourselves (church). The neck of the glass is a paragraph announcement of the Good News. The bottom of the glass, the second half of each sermon, announces salvation, first in the renewal of discipleship (upper bottom), and second in the vision of cultural transformation (lower bottom). In the design, the hourglass figure, the sermon is traced with or without the sermon.

Second, various rhetorical modes and devices are on display in this collection. Below is a simple outline of David Buttrick's recent, excellent preaching textbook. Examples of most of his concepts, noted here, are found in the sermons collected above.

# In the Depths of the Depression
# Sermons 1993

## Design

                                        Cultural Foci

                GOSPEL

Challenge to Disciple

                                    Renewal of Disciple

Cultural
    Transformation

                      ■ Vision
                ■ Invitation to Discipleship

## Tools in the Preacher's Workshop
(from David Buttrick, *Homiletic*, 1988)
1. Structural Modes:
    a. Immediacy
    b. Reflection
    c. Praxis
2. Hermeneutical Proposals:
    a. Community
    b. Duality
    c. Symbolism
3. Moves/Points:
    a. Theological Understanding
    b. Opposition
    c. Real Experience
4. Points/Warning:
    a. Point of View
    b. Transition
    c. Start/Stop
5. Images:
    a. Analogy
    b. Denial
    c. Interpretation
6. Style:
    a. Concrete
    b. -(Adjective)
    c. Pronouns
    d. Personal Active
7. Rhetorical Forms:
    a. Bringing Out
    b. Associating
    c. Disassociating
8. Rhetorical Orientations:
    a. Spatial
    b. Temporal
    c. Personal
    d. Social

## Endnotes

1. John Bartlett, *Familiar Quotations* 15th Edition (Boston: Little, Brown, 1980) p. 857

2. *Ibid.*, p. 346

3. *Ibid.*, p. 890

4. *Ibid.*, p. 891

5. *Ibid.*, p. 909

6. In Central New York, since 1980, three magnificent public buildings have been built. Syracuse University built the Carrier Dome, a sports stadium which seats 60,000, in 1981. Pyramid Corporation built the Carousel Mall, the third largest shopping center in New York State, in 1991 (now referred to by youth and adults simply as "the" mall, although there are a dozen other shopping centers in the area). The Oneida Nation built the Turning Stone Casino in 1993, which gambling center produces more than $1 million of tax-free revenue a day: the multi-million dollar complex was paid for within six months of its opening.

7. *New York Times Magazine,* July 17, 1994: "A Nation of Gamblers"

8. Sara Anne Wood is a teenage girl, daughter of a Presbyterian minister from Utica, New York, who mysteriously disappeared in the summer of 1993. She has not been found.

9. A recent pronouncement from the more conservative, southern wing of The United Methodist Church. Durham refers to Durham, North Carolina.

11. Ralph Harper, *On Presence* (New York: Trinity Press International, 1992) p. 130

12. *The Ante-Nicene Fathers* Vol. 2 (Buffalo: Christian Literature Publishing, 1885) p. 312

13. *Ibid.,* Vol. 1, pp. 376, 384

14. John Wesley, *Explanatory Notes Upon the New Testament* (New York: Eaton) p. 562

15. John Calvin, *Calvin's Commentaries,* trans. T. A. Smail (Grand Rapids: Eerdmans, 1964) p. 394

16. Bartlett, p. 802

17. *Ibid.,* p. 578

18. *Ibid.,* p. 705

19. Abraham Lincoln, Second Inaugural Address

20. Martin Luther, *On Christian Liberty*

21. Bartlett, p. 576

22. *Newscope,* United Methodist News

23. Bartlett, p. 890

24. H. Grady David, *Design for Preaching* (Nashville: Abingdon, 1963)
    David Buttrick, *Homiletic: Moves and Structures* (Philadelphia: Fortress, 1988)

www.ingramcontent.com/pod-product-compliance
Lightning Source LLC
Chambersburg PA
CBHW070933160426
43193CB00011B/1676